Come Ye Yourselves Apart

Our Love and Loyalty Shown in the Day We Rest

J. Lee

Copyright © 2010 by J. Lee

Printed in U.S.A.

All rights reserved.

Layout and design by Greg Solie • AltamontGraphics.com

All Scripture quotations are taken from the King James Version Bible unless noted otherwise.

Table of Contents

Dedication 5

More Than an Introduction 7

1. What Is the Sabbath and Where Did It Come From? 9

2. When God said, "Remember" 13

3. The Sabbath When Jesus Came 17

4. The Sabbath After Christ's Death and Resurrection 21

5. The Origin of Christian Sunday Worship 25

6. The Deciding Mark 29

7. If Not Sunday, What Then? 33

8. God's Law Is a Transcript of His Character 35

9. True Love Will Obey 37

10. Specific Verses Addressed 39

    • Matthew 28:1 39

    • Mark 16:2 39

    • Luke 24:1 39

    • John 20:1 40

    • Mark 16:9 40

    • John 20:19 41

    • Acts 20:7, 11 41

    • 1 Corinthians 16:2 42

    • Colossians 2:14, 16, 17 43

    • Hebrews 3:7-4:11 44

Come Ye Yourselves Apart

11. It Is Finished 49
12. Does Faith Make Void the Law? 51
13. Faulty Promises. 55
14. Abraham and the Covenants 61
15. Sunday and the New Covenant 65
16. Forthright Admissions. .69
17. A Glance at the Imminent Future 75
18. Keeping the Sabbath Holy. 77
19. The Sabbath in a Nutshell 81
Appendix 87
Bibliography 93

**Dedicated most of all to God,
Who made it all possible.
May everything shared be to His honor.
And to you, the reader.
May you be richly blessed.**

*Special thanks to Tom.
Without your questions this book would have never been.*

*Mom,
for all your patient time, advice and proof-reading.*

*Dad and Mom,
I cannot thank you enough for all you have taught and made me.*

Thank you also to

*Marcia Harycki
for the time and effort you put into editing, and for your
patience in explaining the rules of writing to me.*

*Sheree Ruff,
for all your troubleshooting help.
I would probably still be trying to figure it out if it hadn't been for you.*

Thanks to all those who proofread, encouraged and counseled.

More Than an Introduction

What is the Sabbath? Where did it come from? To whom was it given? Does it have any meaning or application to me personally? Has its historical and spiritual significance been lost sight of in the last few centuries?

Where did Sunday worship come from? Is it a legitimate Sabbath substitute? Who is right: my church or the Bible? Have *you* found yourself asking these questions? If you have, you're not alone. Many today are asking these and many other questions; and best of all, they are finding the answers! Where? In God's authoritative Word, the Bible.

I have been asked some of these questions, and have at times asked them myself. This has led me to dig deeper into the Bible and history. My goal was to discover how the Sabbath came to be, how it was observed through the years, if it had any claim on my life, and what its future will be. I was amazed at the wealth of information available as I studied this fascinating subject, and with this illimitable amount of information, I can only highlight a few points.

Why would we want to study such a heavy and controversial subject as the Sabbath? Many people are living life as if it were an endless racetrack. Life is so busy and full, yet people are filled with an overwhelming emptiness. They want to get away from it all, to be alone. They long for time to let their souls catch up to them. This is the purpose of the Sabbath. Jesus calls to every such one, "Come ye yourselves apart…and rest a while" (Mark 6:31). This is why the Sabbath is so crucial in this present time. It is on this day, more than on any other, that our relationships with God and each other can be most effectively formed and strengthened.

Now, if you will, pull up a chair and open up your Bible with me as together we delve into God's Word. We will be comparing Scripture with Scripture, and line with line, peeking into a few old history books now and then as well. Let's see if we can find God's answers to our questions. In the process we may just find something else too. Do you want to know what it is? We will discover a deeper love and appreciation for the God who loves us so much that He sets aside time to come and spend with us each week. Are you comfortable? Good! Then let's begin with a prayer.

"Heavenly Father, thank You for loving us and for wanting to spend intimate time with us. Help me and this dear reader to hear Your voice speaking to us. Open our eyes to behold wondrous things out of Your Word. May You be with us now through the person of the Holy Spirit. And may our hearts be fully yielded to You just now. Thank You, Father, for answering our prayer. In the name of Jesus, Your Son, we pray. Amen."

Chapter 1

What Is the Sabbath and Where Did It Come From?

The Sabbath means different things to different people. To some it means a day to go to church. To others it is a day to kick back and relax or spend time with the family. To still others it means nothing at all. Some say that the Sabbath is an hour at church, while others argue that it is an entire day dedicated to prayer and consecration. Most call Sunday, the first day of the week, Sabbath. Some call Saturday, the seventh day of the week, Sabbath. Still others worship on yet another day of the week. Who is right? Does it even matter if, when, how, and for how long the Sabbath is observed? Are there any answers to this cacophony of beliefs?

Yes! Thankfully, there are. Let us start at the beginning, in the Garden of Eden, back in Genesis. Here we will find both which day is the Sabbath and how the Sabbath came about.

> "And on the seventh day God ended his work which he had made; and he rested on the seventh day from all his work which he had made. And God blessed the seventh day, and sanctified it: because that in it he had rested from all his work which God created and made." Genesis 2:2, 3

God created the Sabbath for man as a memorial of creation. Keep in mind that God did not create Jews at this time, but mankind. In fact, Christ said in Mark 2:27, 28:

> "... The sabbath was made for *man*, and not man for the sabbath: therefore the Son of man is Lord also of the sabbath." (emphasis supplied)

Notice the verse says *man*, not Jews, but man, all humankind—Jews and Gentiles alike. The Sabbath is for all who will yield themselves completely to God as their Creator.

When the Jews did become a nation we find that the Sabbath was part of their belief in and worship of the only True God in a foreign land before the Ten Commandments were given at Sinai. But when they became slaves their work made it difficult to continue this worship and many or all of them became careless. When God called Moses to deliver them, the Children of Israel were laboring almost constantly. Moses met with them and told them that the Lord wanted to free them and apparently he admonished them to return to the worship of God (see Exodus 4:29-31). We know this because when Moses came to Pharaoh with the demand for the release of Israel, the Pharaoh complains saying,

"Wherefore do ye, Moses and Aaron, let the people from their works? Get you unto your burdens. ... Behold, the people of the land now are many, and ye make them rest (*shabath*) from their burdens." Exodus 5:4, 5

The Hebrew word *Shabath*, here translated as *rest,* is the Hebrew root for the word *Shabbath* or Sabbath in English. This root word is used many times in referring to the Biblical Sabbath of the seventh day (Genesis 2:2, 3; Exodus 13:30; 23:12; 31:17; 34:21). The Pharaoh was angry because the people were taking time away from their work to worship God on His Sabbath. The Sabbath was and still is an integral part of the worship of the true God.

As you remember, Pharaoh gave the people extra work to keep them from resting or thinking about leaving Egypt. But through a series of miracles, God brought His people out and led them through the wilderness. He covered them with a cloud of shade by day and warmed them with a pillar of fire at night. He brought water from the rock and rained bread from heaven on them daily—well, almost daily.

Every morning, manna laid on the ground in abundance, but the people were instructed to collect only what they could eat in that day. If they saved any over to the next day it became putrid and filled with worms. Yet on Fridays, God sent extra manna and told the people to gather twice as much. The next day was the Sabbath and no manna would fall on that day.

What Is the Sabbath and Where Did It Come From?

Friday they must save over enough for the next day. God provided another weekly miracle. The manna was still fresh, sweet, and beautiful on Sabbath.

"To morrow is the rest of the holy sabbath unto the Lord: ... that which remaineth over lay up for you to be kept until the morning. And they laid it up till the morning, as Moses bade: and it did not stink, neither was there any worm therein. And Moses said, Eat that today; for today is a Sabbath unto the Lord: to day ye shall not find it in the field. Six days ye shall gather it; but on the seventh day, which is the Sabbath, in it there shall be none." Exodus 16:23-26

Again, even before the Ten Commandments were given from the Mount, God impressed the significance and importance of the Sabbath on His people. For forty years God repeated the miracle and every Sabbath—*2,080 times*—God unmistakably proclaimed the seventh day as the Sabbath.

Chapter 2

When God Said, "Remember"

You may have noticed that in Exodus, when God gave the Ten Commandments to the Children of Israel, He began the fourth one by saying, "Remember." For God to be able to say, "Remember the Sabbath," the people must have had previous knowledge of it. Just as the other nine commandments had been binding, although unwritten long before Sinai, so was the one dealing with the Sabbath.

In the Ten Commandments God again points to creation as one reason to remember the Sabbath.

> "Remember the sabbath day, to keep it holy ... For in six days the LORD made heaven and earth, the sea, and all that in them is, and rested the seventh day: wherefore the LORD blessed the sabbath day and hallowed it." Exodus 20:8, 11

Did you notice something significant there? Aren't we often told that as long as we worship on one day it doesn't really matter to God which day we choose? But in both Exodus and Genesis it says very plainly the seventh and the Sabbath, signifying that there is a very specific day. Indeed, God does care about when we worship.

But there is another sense in which God uses the phrase, "Remember to keep." Suppose you were to come to my house. We visit pleasantly until I am called away for a few hours. You decide to stay until I get back so as I bid you good-bye I add, "Remember to keep the fire going!" Presently you go into the lounge room to put more wood on the fire, only to discover an immaculately clean, cold hearth— the fire had never been started. You cannot "keep" the fire going because it has not been started.

13

When God said "Remember the Sabbath day, to keep it holy" (Exodus 20:8), it was in the context that the seventh day was already sacred. We can only keep or perpetuate its sacredness because it is sacred.

> "And on the seventh day God ended his work which he had made; and he rested on the seventh day from all his work which he had made. And God blessed the seventh day, and sanctified it: because that in it he had rested from all his work which God created and made." Genesis 2:2, 3

Since creation, the seventh day of the week has been sacred. What we do or do not do on that special day does not at all change the sanctity of the day. But what we do or fail to do does change whether or not we can receive the blessing— the sanctity available to us only on this specific day. Of course, there is always a blessing when we spend time with our Lord, which we should do daily, but the Sabbath has a special blessing to which no other day can approach. It is because God so desperately longs to bless us that He commands us to keep His day holy. Listen to His plea,

> "If thou turn away thy foot from the sabbath, from doing thy pleasure on my holy day; and call the sabbath a delight, the holy of the LORD, honourable; and shalt honour him, not doing thine own ways, nor finding thine own pleasure, nor speaking thine own words: Then shalt thou delight thyself in the LORD; and I will cause thee to ride upon the high places of the earth, and feed thee with the heritage of Jacob thy father: for the mouth of the LORD hath spoken it." Isaiah 58:13, 14

Can't you hear His longing to bless? We are His pride and He wants nothing more than to lavish us with Himself. He can only do that when we walk in reverence and obedience to Him. Now just in case you might think He is offering this solely to natural Jews, He gave the following verses a few chapters previous, clearly speaking of the Sabbath, so all mankind would be embraced:

> "Blessed is the man that doeth this, and the son of man that layeth hold on it; that keepeth the sabbath from polluting it, and keepeth

When God Said, "Remember"

his hand from doing any evil. Neither let the son of the *stranger*, that hath joined himself to the Lord, speak, saying, The Lord hath utterly separated me from his people: neither let the *eunuch* say, Behold, I am a dry tree. For thus saith the Lord unto the eunuchs that keep my sabbaths, and choose the things that please me, and take hold of my covenant; Even unto them will I give in mine house and within my walls a place and a name better than of sons and of daughters: I will give them an everlasting name, that shall not be cut off. Also the sons of the *stranger*, that join themselves to the Lord, to serve him, and to love the name of the Lord, to be his servants, every one that keepeth the sabbath from polluting it, and taketh hold of my covenant; Even them will I bring to my holy mountain, and make them joyful in my house of prayer: their burnt offerings and their sacrifices shall be accepted upon mine altar; for mine house shall be called an house of prayer for all people. The Lord God which gathereth the *outcasts* of Israel saith, Yet will I gather others to him, beside those that are gathered unto him." Isaiah 56:2-8 (emphasis supplied)

The blessings are for all who will choose the things that please God, who serve and love Him, keep His Sabbath, and seize His covenant. He asks the same of us as He does of natural Jews. And He offers us equally as rich benefits as He offered to Israel.

It is interesting that the only commandment that God gave us special instruction to remember, is the only commandment the vast majority of professed Protestantism emphatically tells us to forget! Why do we want to preclude God's richest blessings? Rather, let us do all in our power to honor our Father in all things and solicit from His lips,

"Well done, thou good and faithful servant: thou has been faithful over a few things, I will make thee ruler over many things: enter thou into the joy of thy lord." Matthew 25:21

Chapter 3

The Sabbath When Jesus Came

At the time of Christ, Israel had lost sight of the true meaning of the temple, its services and ceremonial laws. Even the laws that had ruled man from the very beginning of time, the Ten Commandments, were misunderstood. The religious leaders taught that keeping rules was the way to be saved and that the more rules a person kept, the holier they would be. In essence, they taught salvation by works. They made their own laws, and while God's true laws were distorted and forgotten, the man-made, tyrannical laws were accredited to God. These were regarded as the highest standards of holiness. This made God seem exacting, cruel and One whose demands could not be satisfied. Jesus Himself spoke to this, saying to the scribes and Pharisees;

> "…Why do ye also transgress the commandment of God by your tradition?…But in vain they do worship me, teaching for doctrines the commandments of men." Matthew 15:3, 9

This is the scene upon which Christ entered. It was His privilege to show to us, in human form, that God, His Father, was a God of love, and that He does not ask of us more than we are capable of giving. It became paramount for Christ to vindicate the law of God. Through His life, Christ showed that the law of God is just, and that it can be obeyed. He said,

> "Think not that I am come to destroy the law: … I am not come to destroy, but to fulfill." Matthew 5:17

What does the word "fulfill" mean? Some suggest that Christ is saying He didn't come to destroy the law but to do away with it, but that would be a contradiction. He must have meant something else. Let's see what some synonyms of fulfill might be: perform, discharge, bring into effect, execute. The second definition for this word in the dictionary says, "to perform or do, as duty; obey or follow, as commands."[1] This is the way Christ was using the word fulfill.

In no way was Jesus saying that the Ten Commandments had no more value or that they could be changed. If the law could have been changed, He would not have needed to come to this world, because the law could have simply been re-written so that man could still be saved in his sinful state. But no, this could not be done. God's law was perfect; there was no way it could, or needed to, be changed. The law must and can be obeyed through God's strength. It is not a means of obtaining salvation, but is evidence of God's saving us from our worst enemy of sin and self.

Christ obeyed the laws of His Heavenly Father in every particular, including the Sabbath! It is no secret that He was careful in observing the Sabbath. The Bible gives us many examples. Let us look at just a few of them.

"And they [Jesus and His apostles] went into Capernaum; and straightway on the sabbath day he [Jesus] entered into the synagogue, and taught." Mark 1:21

"And he [Jesus] came to Nazareth, where he had been brought up: and, *as his custom was*, he went into the synagogue on the Sabbath day, and stood up for to read." Luke 4:16 (emphasis supplied)

"And it came to pass also on another sabbath, that he [Jesus] entered into the synagogue and taught." Luke 6:6

Thus we see that during Jesus' life, He unfailingly kept the Sabbath sacred, indicating in no way by example or word that the Sabbath was to be discontinued or that its solemnity was to be transferred to another day. While the Jews had made the day one of bondage, of do's and don'ts, Jesus restored it to it's original intent. It was to be a day of holy joy, peaceful communion with our Father and Creator, and a day to share that joy, hope, help and fortitude in God in an even more special way with others. In Scripture

The Sabbath When Jesus Came

we often find Christ relieving, or referring to relieving, the emotional, spiritual or physical needs of man and animal on the Sabbath.

Jesus, as if to insure that we not misinterpret any act or statement during His life, was careful of the sacredness of the Sabbath, even in His death! Luke tells us that, "...and there was a darkness over all the earth until the ninth hour" (which would be approximately 3 p.m.), shortly after which "... he gave up the ghost" Luke 23:44, 46. Jesus' disciples took His body down and tenderly "... wrapped it in linen, and laid it in a sepulchre that was hewn in stone, wherein never man before was laid. And that day was the preparation, and the sabbath drew on. ... And they returned, and prepared spices and ointments; and rested the sabbath day according to the commandment" Luke 23:53, 54, 56.

> "Now upon the first day of the week, very early in the morning, they [the women] came unto the sepulchre. ... And they found the stone rolled away from the sepulchre. And they entered in, and found not the body of the Lord Jesus." Luke 24:1-3

Jesus died, ending the first phase of saving man prior to sundown Friday, leaving His beloved disciples enough time to perform the necessary burial rites and prepare themselves for the Sabbath before its sacred hours began. His work to that point was accomplished. During those preciously close and hallowed hours, He rested peacefully in the tomb, under His Father's loving watch-care. Then early Sunday morning His Father called Him from His peaceful repose, to begin the mediatorial phase of redeeming man. Yes, even in His death, Christ kept the Sabbath holy! Thus, through Jesus' death and resurrection, the Sabbath becomes not only a sign of God's creative power, but also of His redemptive power.

NOTE:

It is also worthy of notice that Luke says:

> "... they returned...and rested the sabbath day according to *the commandment.*" Luke 23:56

Come Ye Yourselves Apart

It doesn't say, "according to the *custom*" or "tradition." It says, "According to *the commandment.*" It is the fourth of the same Ten Commandment law spoken with thunder from the mouth of God, and written indelibly in stone with His own finger, that Luke is referring to, not some tradition or custom of men, but the eternal, loving law of God.

The Commandments were given by the kind and loving God, Who desires a personal relationship with each of us individually. While God longs to be real and personal every day of the week, the Sabbath affords a special opportunity to get especially close without the demands of everyday life.

Chapter 4

The Sabbath after Christ's Death and Resurrection

Did Christ's disciples continue to keep the seventh day Sabbath after His death and resurrection? Is it even possible to know? Indeed it is! Let's take a look at what Luke tells us in the book of Acts.

"But when [Paul and his friends] departed from Perga, they came to Antioch in Pisidia, and went into the synagogue on the Sabbath day, and sat down. ... And when the Jews were gone out of the synagogue, the Gentiles besought that these words might be preached to them the next sabbath. ... And the next sabbath day came almost the whole city together to hear the word of God." Acts 13:14, 42, 44

Here is another example, from Luke and Paul.

"And on the sabbath we went out of the city by a river side, where prayer was wont to be made; and we sat down, and spake unto the women which resorted thither." Acts 16:13

"And Paul, *as his manner was*, went in unto them, and three sabbath days reasoned with them out of the scriptures." Acts 17:2

"And he [Paul] reasoned in the synagogue every sabbath, and persuaded the Jews and the Greeks." Acts 18:4

It is of interest that even the Gentile Christians (Greeks) kept the Sabbath. It is obvious that there has been no change in days of worship yet,

21

Come Ye Yourselves Apart

and that the keeping holy of the seventh-day Sabbath was inclusive of all humanity, not merely of the Jews.

Now let us move ahead in time to around the year 95 A.D.. John is all alone. He is the only disciple who has personally walked with Jesus and is still alive. He is banished to a little solitary island, the isle of Patmos. But even here in this dreary place, he finds peace in God. He says,

"I was in the Spirit on the Lord's day ..." Revelation 1:10

Which day is the Lord's?

"But the *seventh day* is the sabbath *of the* LORD thy God ..." Exodus 20:10

In Isaiah, God says that the Sabbath is

"... my holy day ..." Isaiah 58:13

In the New Testament, God still calls the seventh-day Sabbath His day:

"For the Son of man is Lord even of the sabbath day." Matthew 12:8

"... the Son of man is Lord also of the sabbath." Luke 6:5

These texts all seem to indicate that the "Lord's day" and the seventh-day Sabbath are the same. In fact, in the Bible, no day other than the Sabbath is called "the Lord's day," except the day of judgment, which clearly does not apply within the context of this passage.

Often the claim is made that by the time John wrote Revelation, Sunday was the normal and accepted day of worship, and that this is the day He was referring to in Revelation 1:10. However, historically, this is woefully incorrect. Sunday worship did not enter the Christian world until around 300 A.D., and even then it was kept along with the seventh-day Sabbath, not in place of it. This being the case, Revelation was written approximately 200-plus years prior to the introduction of Sunday worship into Christianity. It becomes rather apparent that John could not have been

22

The Sabbath After Christ's Death and Resurrection

referring to Sunday as the Lord's day. He could be speaking only of the Sabbath of the Ten Commandments.*

John also was a Sabbath keeper, as were all the Christians at that time. They followed in the example of their Lord Jesus.

In fact, a careful look at the people and their religious beliefs in the past two thousand years or so will reveal that there have always been those who kept the seventh day holy. No other day was sanctified by Christians until some chose to compromise their standards in the latter part of the third century in order to make themselves less conspicuous. Then, in the fourth century, the Roman emperor, Constantine I, established Sunday as the universal day of rest.

In spite of this, however, God's faithful people continued to keep the only true Sabbath of the seventh day holy. God had His allegiant people in all countries at all times. Although they did not understand all that God would have liked them to, they lived up to what they understood at the time. Many of them shared their faith, including the Sabbath, with others, even in the face of certain death (see Appendix 1).

---

* Revelation was written at least a year prior to the gospel of John. At the time John wrote his gospel, he evidently regarded the seventh day as the Sabbath (John 5:9, 10, 16, 18; 7:22, 23; 9:14, 16; 19:31). In Revelation 1:10, if he was calling the first day of the week the Lord's Day, and keeping it sacred, as most wish us to believe, did he change his mind a year later and go back to keeping the true Sabbath? No, he was consistent in his faith. John kept the same seventh-day Sabbath when he wrote Revelation, as he did when he wrote the gospel of John a year later.

Chapter 5

The Origin of Christian Sunday Worship

For approximately 300 years after Christ's resurrection, the seventh-day Sabbath was the only day on which the organized Christians worshiped God. But the Jews were a detested people among the then world government of Rome. Because the Christian believers held many things in common with the Jews such as diet and the Sabbath, they often shared in their persecution. For this reason, Christians sought to distance themselves from the ill-favored Jews and they felt that by christening some pagan practices and making less prominent their Christian beliefs they could not only attain distinction from the Jews but perhaps win some of the pagans to the Church. Both of these goals were accomplished to some degree but not without a high cost— the loss of the sacred truths of Christ and His apostles.

Constantine who began ruling about this time was a worshiper of Sol Invictus, the pagan sun god, while also professing to be a Christian. On March 7, 321, in honor of Sol Invictus, Constantine decreed *dies Solis* (day of the sun, or Sunday) as a day of rest.

> On the venerable day of the Sun let the magistrates and people residing in cities rest, and let all workshops be closed. In the country however persons engaged in agriculture may freely and lawfully continue their pursuits because it often happens that another day is not suitable for grain-sowing or vine planting; lest by neglecting the proper moment for such operations the bounty of heaven should be lost. [CJ3.12.2] M. Wallraff, Christus Verus Sol, 2002, 96-102. [1]

Dies Solis was not a mandated day of worship but a cessation of labor. But thus began the crossing over, the mingling of sacred and common fires (Leviticus 10:1, 2). Many tried vainly to serve both God and man by resting on both days. But God's command to rest on the Seventh day was followed by the equal command to work the other six days. Because many of the Christians attempted to obey God and man they found the burden painfully heavy and eventually these compromising Christians became the leaders of a growing apostate Christian Church.

For those in this young Catholic Church, the solemn, sacred Sabbath, was followed by Sunday, which was a day of fun and festivities. And because God, the Sabbath, and the Jews were looked on through a distorted, embittered light, people gravitated more toward Sunday observance. In the year 336, cannon 29 was formulated by some of the Church leaders and at the Council of Laodicea in 363 it became the official, universal Church mandate. Canon 29 was the primary canon approved at the council of Laodicea. It prohibits resting on Sabbath, Saturday, and compels Christians to sanctify what they call the "Lord's day" or Sunday.

Canon 29
Christians *must not* judaize by resting on the Sabbath, but *must work* on that day, rather honouring the Lord's Day; and, if they can, resting then as Christians. But if any shall be found to be judaizers, let them be anathema from Christ. Nicene and Post-Nicene Fathers, Second Series, Vol. 14 emphasis supplied. [2]

No longer was it just Constantine, a "Christian" Pagan Government Ruler, ordering a day of rest for townsfolk. It was the fast-growing, prominent Church's mandate ordering not just Sunday rest but worship, while **demanding** work and **forbidding** worship on Sabbath.

This powerful Church, while it has done much good, has also consistently and unashamedly undermined some of the most direct commands and teachings of God. Without apology they boast of making the change.

"The Catholic Church ... by virtue of her divine mission, changed the day from Saturday to Sunday." *The Catholic Mirror*, September 23,1893. *[The Mirror is a Baltimore-based Catholic weekly paper]*
"*Question*: Which is the Sabbath day?

The Origin of Christian Sunday Worship

Answer: Saturday is the Sabbath day.
Question: Why do we observe Sunday instead of Saturday?
Answer: We observe Sunday instead of Saturday because the Catholic Church transferred the solemnity from Saturday to Sunday." Peter Geiermann, *The Convert's Catechism of Catholic Doctrine,* 1957 edition, p 50. [3]

"Sunday is a Catholic institution, and its claims to observance can be defended only on Catholic principles. ...From beginning to end of scripture there is not a single passage that warrants the transfer of weekly public worship from the last day of the week to the first." *Catholic Press,* Sydney, Australia, August 1900.

"If we consulted the Bible only, we should still have to keep holy the Sabbath day, that is Saturday." John Laux, *A Course in Religion for Catholic High Schools and Academies,* 1936 edition, Volume 1, p 51.

"If Protestants would follow the Bible, they should worship God on the Sabbath day. In keeping Sunday they are following a law of the Catholic Church." Albert Smith, chancellor of the Archdiocese of Baltimore, replying for the cardinal in a letter dated February 10, 1920.

"Reason and common sense demand the acceptance of one or the other of these alternatives: either Protestantism and the keeping holy of Saturday, or Catholicity and the keeping holy of Sunday. Compromise is impossible." *The Catholic Mirror,* December 23, 1893. [4]

"... The Bible which Protestants claim to obey exclusively, gives no authorization for the substitution of the first day of the week for the seventh. On what authority have they done so? Plainly on the authority of that [same] Catholic Church which they abandoned, and whose traditions they condemn." John L. Stoddard, *Rebuilding a Lost Faith,* p 80.

"Thus we see Daniel 7:25 fulfilled, the little horn changing 'times and laws.' Therefore it appears to me that all who keep the first day for the Sabbath are the Pope's Sunday-keepers, and God's Sabbath breakers." Elder T. M. Preble, American Seventh-day Baptist, Feb. 13, 1845. [5]

* Flavius Valerius Aurelius Constantinus, ("The Great") A.D. 288?-337. Roman emperor from 324-337. [6]

Chapter 6

The Deciding Mark

The Bible tells us that at the end of this earth's history, the two opposing powers in this cosmic conflict of good and evil will have their separate marks of distinction. Incidentally, the Bible uses the words "mark," "seal" and "sign" interchangeably.

"And I saw another angel ascending from the east, having the *seal of the living God*...Saying, Hurt not the earth...till we have *sealed the servants of our God* in their foreheads." Revelation 7:2, 3

"And he [the beast] causeth all, both small and great, rich and poor, free and bond, to receive a mark in their right hand, or in their foreheads: And that no man might buy or sell, save he that had the mark. ..." Revelation 13:16, 17

The Bible also tells us what God's seal is. He says of the Sabbath that,

"It is a sign. ..." Exodus 31:17

"Moreover also I gave them *my sabbaths*, to be a *sign* between me and them, that they might know that I am the LORD that sanctify them. ... And hollow *my sabbaths*; and they shall be a *sign* between me and you, that ye may know that I am the LORD your God." Ezekiel 20:12, 20

In order to be valid a seal must contain three validations proving its authenticity and authority. The three things that validate the seal are: #1,

29

Come Ye Yourselves Apart

it must contain the name of the ruler; #2, the ruler's title; #3, the extent of his realm. For illustration, let's take the queen of England's seal. #1, name: Elizabeth II. #2, title: Queen. #3, realm: United Kingdom. Interestingly, we find that God's seal is found only in the fourth commandment. Watch carefully:

> "For in six days the LORD [name] made [Creator: title] *heaven* and *earth,* the *sea,* and all that in them is [realm], and rested the seventh day: [and because He has that authority and right]...the LORD blessed the sabbath day, and hallowed it" Exodus 20:11

It is obvious then that the Sabbath is God's seal, sign or mark, and our willing adherence to the Sabbath places God's seal in us. When we keep God's Sabbath holy, we become His realm.

However, where there is a genuine, there will also be a false. The Sabbath as God's seal is no exception. The Bible tells us that there is another power that, while professing to love God and doing many wonderful things, will in actuality be opposed to the Word, law, and indeed, in some ways, even the very character of God. If the true Sabbath is God's seal, then the power opposing Him would choose a false Sabbath. That is exactly what it has done, and it proudly boasts the fact, saying:*

> "Of course the Catholic Church claims that the change [of Sabbath to Sunday] was her act... and the *act is a MARK* of her ecclesiastical power." From the office of Cardinal Gibbons, through Chancellor H. F. Thomas, November 11, 1895.

> "Sunday is our *MARK* of authority!...The Church is above the Bible, and this transference of Sabbath observance is proof of that fact." *The Catholic Record,* London, Ontario, Canada, September 1, 1923.

While Protestant churches vehemently condemn Catholicity, they complacently sit by, honoring her mark of authority, and attempt at all costs to defend a day of worship that finds its roots in paganism and has only years of tradition for its defense. Yet Christ said of tradition,

The Deciding Mark

"Howbeit in vain do they worship me, teaching for doctrine the commandments of men. ... Full well ye reject the commandment of God, that ye may keep your own tradition. ... Making the word of God of none effect through your tradition..." Mark 7:7, 9, 13

NOTE:

In Ezekiel 20:12, 20 it is interesting to note what God says is the reason for the Sabbath. It is so:

"... that they might know that I am the LORD that sanctify them ... that ye may know that I am the LORD your God."

The Sabbath is for us, so that we will not forget who our Lord is, and Who it is that sanctifies us. The Sabbath is for our benefit, to focus our attention on our Creator, Redeemer, Restorer and Friend. Without spending this sacred time with Him on His day, and in His way, He knew that we would all too quickly forget Who it was that made us, and Who it is that saves us. This is why He said for us to "remember," and this is why it is His seal, showing to all that we are His, both by creation and redemption.

---

*Please! Remember that just as there is wonderful truth in every church, so there are also some very serious falsehoods as well. The majority of most church members, and even their clergy, are innocently unaware of these Biblical inconsistencies. Therefore, it behooves us to be gentle. Truth, even when presented in a most delicate way, is very sharp and discomfiting. Jesus said plainly that He had many sheep that were in other folds, meaning that His people are not those of any one particular denomination, but those who are yielded to Him and are desiring to know and do His will.

Chapter 7

If Not Sunday, What Then?

When asked why they sanctify Sunday, most Protestants answer that it is a memorial of Christ's resurrection. They say that since His death, Christians have always observed that day. But this is not the case, as we have already shown. Sunday-keeping did not come into existence for nearly 300 years after Christ's death. It was set up purely on the foundation of paganism, not as a reminder of Christ's resurrection.

The resurrection is very important. If Christ had not risen, we would still be lost and without hope of ever entering Heaven. If Christ had not risen, it would mean that He failed in some point; therefore, needed a savior Himself! But, praise God, He did rise, and this certainly is an event worthy of remembrance. God definitely would not want us to lose sight of it.

So if Sunday is not the memorial of the resurrection, what is? Listen as Paul tells us.

> "Buried with him in *baptism,* wherein also ye are risen with him through the faith of the operation of God, who hath raised him from the dead." Colossians 2:12. Emphasis supplied

> "Know ye not, that so many of us as were baptized into Jesus Christ were baptized into his death? Therefore we are buried with him by baptism into death: that like as Christ was raised up from the dead by the glory of the Father, even so we also should walk in newness of life." Romans 6:3, 4

The word *baptizo* means "to immerse," which is exactly how Christ was baptized (see Mark 1:9, 10). This is also the way the Apostles baptized

33

(see Acts 8:36, 38, 39). Biblical baptism is a complete immersion in water. This type of baptism is a perfect reminder of Christ's death and burial (being lowered into the water), and of His resurrection (being raised up out of the water). This is a very solemn and important event, because it points back to the time Jesus paid the ultimate price for all. Baptism means death to sin, and resurrection to a new life in Christ!

NOTE:

On a smaller scale, the foot washing and communion services are also reminders of Jesus' death, burial and resurrection. Both services call us to put away self, pride and sin. In communion, the unleavened bread symbolizes accepting Jesus Christ into the heart through prayer and His Word. The unfermented grape juice represents His shed blood, which means eternal life for you and me.

Chapter 8

God's Law Is a Transcript of His Character

In the law we find God's character. You see, throughout the Bible, God and the law are described with the same adjectives: good, holy and just. Sin has separated us from God and has distorted our perceptions of Him. Our sin made God look cruel and exacting, and it is the same sin that makes the law seem harsh and demanding. But God did not change when we sinned! He was the same loving God who loved us and longed to dwell with us. This is why He wrote out the Ten Commandments. He wanted us to see Him as He truly is. But, somehow, sin has so blinded our eyes that the very manner in which God meant to show us His love has been interpreted to be just the opposite!

Does our failure to understand the law's real meaning make it any less loving and kind? No, not any more than our failure to understand God makes Him unloving and cruel. When my heart is surrendered to God, and He is allowed to have complete control of my life, then I see His love in His individualized care for me. Because I am completely surrendered to Him I can see the beauty of His character as recorded in His loving law.

Let's suppose I wrote out a description of my character. If someone changed the document, would that make any change in who I am? Not at all. But it would affect their understanding of me. They would never be able to truly get to know me the way I am, because they would be assuming that my character is something other than what it is.

This is precisely what we have done with God. He wrote out His character, and we have come in and changed things. Now this has not changed God at all, but it has affected our ability to get to know Him. God is still the same. Sin still cannot enter His presence, any more than those breaking the law can stand in its shadow without feeling its crushing weight. To say that the law is no longer needed is to say that God is no longer needed! Both must come together; they are inseparable; one and the same. Because God's law is an expression of Himself, it cannot be changed or abolished without changing or abolishing God!

"And it is easier for heaven and earth to pass, than one tittle of the law to fail." Luke 16:17

Attributes	God Is	His Law Is
Good	Luke 18:191	Timothy 1:8
Holy	Isaiah 5:16	Romans 7:12
Perfect	Matthew 5:48	Psalms 19:7
Pure	1 John 3:2, 3	Psalms 19:8
Just	Deuteronomy 32:4	Romans 7:12
True	John 3:33	Psalms 119:142
Spiritual	1 Corinthians 10:4	Romans 7:14
Righteous	Psalms 145:17	Psalms 119:172
Faithful	1 Corinthians 1:9	Psalms 119:86
Love	1 John 4:8	Romans 13:10
Unchanging	James 1:17	Matthew 5:18
Everlasting	Genesis 21:33	Psalms 111:7, 8

Chapter 9

True Love Will Obey

The Bible tells us that those who love God will obey Him.

"And hereby we do know that we know him, if we keep his commandments. ... He that saith he abideth in him ought himself also so to walk, even as he walked." 1 John 2:3, 6

"For this is the love of God, that we keep his commandments: and his commandments are not grievous." 1 John 5:3

"And this is love, that we walk after his commandments…" 2 John 6

It is love for God because of what He has done to save us that will compel us to obey Him. In fact, in Revelation we are told that those who will enter Heaven will be ones who have obeyed God's law.

"Here is the patience of the saints: here are *they* that *keep the commandments of God*, and the faith of Jesus." Revelation 14:12

"Blessed are they that *do His commandments*, that they may have right to the tree of life, and may enter in through the gates into the city." Revelation 22:14

In Isaiah, God specifically says that we will still be observing the Sabbath of the fourth commandment in Heaven.

Come Ye Yourselves Apart

"And it shall come to pass, that…from one sabbath to another, shall all flesh come to worship before me, saith the LORD." Isaiah 66:23

NOTE:

In chapter one, *"What is the Sabbath, and Where did it Come From?"*, we saw that the Sabbath is a sign of God's <u>creative</u> power, as seen in the institution of the Sabbath at the time of Creation.

Chapter three, *"The Sabbath When Jesus Came"*, showed us the Sabbath as a sign of God's <u>redemptive</u> power as seen by His careful completion of the sacrificial aspect of saving man before the Sabbath hours began, and His resuming the mediatorial aspect of redeeming man soon after His resurrection on Sunday.

Finally, in *"True Love Will Obey"*, we've learned that the Sabbath is also a sign of God's <u>re-creative</u> power as seen by the continuance of Sabbath observance in Heaven and the New Earth. There, as in the Garden of Eden, we will talk face to face with God as we spend those hallowed hours sitting at His feet, perhaps under the tree of life. There He will reveal to us the plan of salvation and how He worked specifically to save you and me individually.

Chapter 10

Specific Verses Addressed

Many times very vital truths are missed and people are led to false conclusions simply by not taking the time to carefully consider the true meaning of a verse in its context. The subject of the Sabbath is one of these vital truths that has been missed by drawing faulty conclusions from verses that have either been looked at too quickly or out of context. Let's spend the next few minutes carefully studying these some times misapplied verses. To begin, let us look at the eight times that Sunday or the first day of the week is referred to. Let's see if Sunday's sacredness is ever inferred.

Matthew 28:1

"In the end of the sabbath, as it began to dawn toward the first day of the week, came Mary Magdalene and the other Mary to see the sepulchre."

Mark 16:2

"And very early in the morning the first day of the week, they came unto the sepulchre at the rising of the sun."

Luke 24:1

"Now upon the first day of the week, very early in the morning, they came unto the sepulchre, bringing the spices which they had prepared, and certain others with them."

John 20:1

"The first day of the week cometh Mary Magdalene early, when it was yet dark, unto the sepulchre, and seeth the stone taken away from the sepulchre."

Each of these four texts refers to the first day of the week, Sunday, as a common working day. Each of the persons mentioned in these texts rested the Sabbath as Christ had shown them by His own example. On the first day of the week they promptly resumed their work where they had left off the Friday evening before. One will find absolutely no inference in these texts that Sunday was being or is to be kept, holy. The women were not going to early morning Sunday service at the temple. No indeed, they were going about the usual weekly activities that they had rested from during the Sabbath hours.

Mark 16:9

"Now when Jesus was risen early the first day of the week, he appeared first to Mary Magdalene, out of whom he had cast seven devils."

In total abandonment to overwhelming grief, Mary lingered near the place where she had last seen her Lord. In love and compassion, Jesus came to her and asked,

"Woman, why weepest thou? whom seekest thou?"

Not recognizing Him and thinking He was the gardener, she asked if He had moved the body of her Lord, demanding that, if so, He show her where Jesus was placed. Then Jesus said her name. Instantly she realized Who was talking with her and flinging herself at His feet, she cried, "Master!" Very tenderly, Jesus said,

"Touch me not; for I am not yet ascended to my Father: but go to My brethren, and say unto them, I ascend unto my Father, and to your Father; and to my God, and to your God."

Specific Verses Addressed

There is no conversation here as to the new sacredness of Sunday. Christ's only concern is for His followers. He wants them to know that He loves them and that they are not alone. (This discourse can be found in John 20:15-17.)

John 20:19

"Then the same day at evening, being the first day of the week, when the doors were shut where the disciples were assembled for fear of the Jews, came Jesus and stood in the midst, and saith unto them, Peace be unto you."

Again, out of tender love and His desire to comfort the sorrowing disciples, Jesus comes to them. In the ensuing dissertation, Jesus verifies that He is indeed the same One that they have loved and followed and buried and that He has truly risen from the dead. He also gives them insight into their future occupation as His witnesses. But never once in the five-verse discussion does He even hint at Sunday being a day of worship. He doesn't even imply that it is in any way made holy by His resurrection. Nor does He say that it is at any time to be made a day of special remembrance.

Acts 20:7, 11

"And upon the first day of the week, when the disciples came together to break bread, Paul preached unto them, ready to depart on the morrow; and continued his speech until midnight. ... When he therefore was come up again, and had broken bread, and eaten, and talked a long while, even till break of day, so he departed."

This verse can be understood in two ways, neither of which support the claim that this was a typical Sunday church service. The days in Biblical times were always figured from sundown to sundown (see Leviticus 23:32; Deuteronomy 16:6; Nehemiah 13:19; Mark 1:21,32). What we would call Saturday night was, to them, the beginning of Sunday. And what, to us, would be Sunday night would be to them the beginning of Monday. Therefore, this was most likely an extra Saturday night meeting so the believers could have one last chance to hear Paul before he left Sunday morning. It began shortly after the sun had set. They ate supper together, then Paul began to preach to them one last time. Getting long-winded (to the near demise of one of his listeners), he preached until early Sunday morning.

An alternate explanation is that this could have been a late Sunday afternoon supper and meeting that went on through most of the night, meaning that the majority of the meeting would have been on Monday. Either way, it was not the usual timing for their worship services and thus does not in any way denote sacredness of that day.

1 Corinthians 16:2

"Upon the first day of the week let every one of you lay by him in store, as God hath prospered him, that there be no gatherings when I come."

There are two key phrases in this verse that make the meaning clear if they are not skipped over too quickly. They are (1) "… let every one lay *by him* …" and (2) "…*in store*, …" Each individual was to lay up his offering at home, by himself, alone, except for God. The gifts were to be set aside on a weekly basis according as God had blessed him. Then, when Paul came, they would be given publicly.

This accomplished two things: first, because they were planning ahead and weekly setting aside the gifts, they were able to give more than if they had to try to find something at the last moment. Second, this method was also more expedient, in that Paul would not be staying long, and if the gifts were already prepared they could be easily brought without delaying Paul's journey. But these initial gatherings were not done in public or at a weekly Sunday service. They were to be at home, alone, and then on whatever day Paul arrived, they would be given openly.

There is no Sunday worship being incorporated here. Paul is not telling them to come together to worship and give money. No. At home they were to save up whatever gifts they could give in order to relieve the wants of the believers suffering from the famine at Jerusalem. (Acts 11:27-30 and Romans 15:25, 26 refer to this widespread—throughout the Jewish world—famine. Josephus dates this famine at approximately 44-47 ce and lasting 3-4 years with the result of intense suffering and copious deaths.)

Specific Verses Addressed

Colossians 2:14, 16, 17

"Blotting out the *handwriting* of *ordinances* that was against us, which was contrary to us, and took it out of the way, nailing it to his cross…Let no man therefore judge you in meat, or in drink, or in respect of an holyday, or of the new moon, or of the sabbath days: *Which are a shadow of things to come…*"

Again, there are two things that must not be missed if we are going to have a correct understanding of what Paul is saying to us. The first thing we notice is that Paul is talking about the handwriting of ordinances. What were the handwritten ordinances that the Jews held so highly? Were they the same as the Ten Commandments?

The ceremonial laws containing the laws and rights for the sanctuary system were written by Moses.

"And Moses wrote all the words of the LORD, and rose up early in the morning, and builded an altar under the hill, and twelve pillars, according to the twelve tribes of Israel." Exodus 24:4

In another place, God refers to these ceremonial laws as being written by Moses. He says that He will punish Israel

"… so that they will take heed to do all that I have commanded them, according to the whole law (the Ten Commandments) and the statutes and the ordinances *by the hand of Moses* (the ceremonial laws)." 2 Chronicles 33:8

While God spoke the Ten Commandments with thunder, He wrote them in stone with His own finger, signifying their endurance and unfailing validity. But the laws regarding the sanctuary service were written on parchment by Moses under God's direction. These were intended to last only until they had been completed in Christ and then they would be no longer binding. These laws were commonly referred to as "handwritten," clarifying to all which law was being discussed.

The best clarification for our texts in Colossians is at the very end of verse 17. The phrase is: *"which are a shadow of things to come."* So the way of eating and drinking, the holy days, the new moon, and the Sabbath days mentioned, all pointed to something or someone that was to come in the future. When the One to whom all these things had pointed had come, there was no longer any need for the symbol. These things had nothing to do with the Ten Commandments. These were entirely different laws, having to do with the sanctuary system and the theocracy form of government.

The Jews had many festivals that were called Sabbaths, some of which lasted many days such as the Feast of Tabernacles, or Booths, the Day of Atonement, the Feast of Trumpets, and the Sabbatical Year. All of these pointed to something yet to come or to take place. Thus, after Christ's life, death, and resurrection, these festivals and sabbaths were of no further significance.

However, the weekly Sabbath of the Ten Commandments is all-encompassing, past, present, and future. It is never outdated. It is perfectly situated to care for the needs of all, in all ages. The Sabbath points back to creation. It reminds us of redemption in the present. The Sabbath betokens our future translation and the recreation of the earth as its reason for existence.

Hebrews 3:7-4:11

To better understand this passage, it is important to understand the underlying premise of the book. In Hebrews, Paul recounts the history of ancient Israel. He presents their experiences as lessons for us today so that we don't make the same mistakes and experience the same setbacks.

In the passage preceding our particular passage of interest, Paul establishes two themes: our committed faithfulness and God's dwelling place. As we look at our passage beginning in verse seven we will discover that Paul continues with these two themes, building on and expanding their scope, and our appreciation. We will also find that Paul binds these two themes inseparably together, bringing us face to face with the Sabbath.

Unfortunately, in the translation from Greek to English some of the intent or meaning of the words was lost. In this particular passage, Paul uses three related but completely different Greek words which were all translated "rest." To make it easier to understand and follow Paul's intent here,

Specific Verses Addressed

I have replaced "rest" with their actual and contextual English meaning. I have indicated these words with bold/italic.

Wherefore (as the Holy Ghost saith, To day if ye will hear his voice, Harden not your hearts, as in the provocation, in the day of temptation in the wilderness: When your fathers tempted me, proved me, and saw my works forty years. Wherefore I was grieved with that generation, and said, They do alway err in their heart; and they have not known my ways. So I sware in my wrath, They shall not enter into my *abode [katapausis]*.) Take heed, brethren, lest there be in any of you an evil heart of unbelief, in departing from the living God. But exhort one another daily, while it is called To day; lest any of you be hardened through the deceitfulness of sin. For we are made partakers of Christ, if we hold the beginning of our confidence steadfast unto the end; While it is said, To day if ye will hear his voice, harden not your hearts, as in the provocation. For some, when they had heard, did provoke: howbeit not all that came out of Egypt by Moses. Hebrews 3:7-16

Paul continues with the emphasis of faithfulness, beseeching us to learn from Israel's lack of faithfulness—their unbelief. Notice how he tactfully weaves entering into God's abode with our unwavering faithfulness.

But with whom was he [God] grieved forty years? was it not with them that had sinned, whose carcases fell in the wilderness? And to whom sware he that they should not enter into his *abode [katapausis]*, but to them that believed not? So we see that they could not enter in because of unbelief. Let us therefore fear, lest, a promise being left us of entering into his *abode [katapausis]*, any of you should seem to come short of it. For unto us was the gospel preached, as well as unto them: but the word preached did not profit them, not being mixed with faith in them that heard it. For we which have believed do enter into [His] *abode [katapausis]* As he said, As I have sworn in my wrath, if they shall enter into my *abode [katapausis]*: although the works were finished from the foundation of the world. For he spake in a certain place of the seventh day on this wise, And God did *desist [katapauo]* the seventh day from all his works. Hebrews 3:17-4:4

Ever so gently Paul makes inseparable the theme of God's abiding place with His requirement of absolute faithfulness on our part in order to enter into that place. While Paul continues with his primary theme of unflinching faithfulness, he begins to broaden his secondary theme and our understanding of what exactly it means to make God our abode. Watch carefully as the next verses take us to the climax:

And in this place again, If they shall enter into my *abode [katapausis]*. Seeing therefore it remaineth that some must enter therein, and they to whom it was first preached entered not in because of unbelief: Again, he limiteth a certain day, saying in David, To day, after so long a time; as it is said, To day if ye will hear his voice, harden not your hearts. For if [Jehoshua] had given them *desist [katapauo]*, then would he not afterward have spoken of another day. Hebrews 4:5-8

A literal and accurate translation of Hebrews 4:8 is

If Jehoshua [Joshua] had ***desisted*** *these things* would he not have *spoken* of a *different day*? [Underlined/italic words are the only words found in the original Greek manuscripts.]

Wait a minute! We have been talking about faithfulness, belief and unbelief and an abiding place in God, where did a "day" come from? Paul is bringing us swiftly to his climax. Very skillfully, he blends the new concept completely in at this juncture. He asks an obvious question, if Joshua had brought an end to this abode in God, wouldn't he have pointed them to something else? The resounding answer is that he didn't bring it to an end! Paul clinches the thought by introducing another completely new word, which is our third usage of "rest," into the discussion.

There remaineth therefore *Sabbath [sabbatismos]* to the people of God. For he that is entered into his [God's] *abode [katapausis]*, he also hath ceased from his own works, as God did from his. Let us

Specific Verses Addressed

labour therefore to enter into that **abode** *[katapausis]*, lest any man fall after the same example of unbelief. Hebrews 4:9-11

Paul brings us to the height of his argument, making inseparable the seventh-day Sabbath with those who faithfully obey God and therefore abide in Him. Those who are unreservedly committed, faithful to God will unquestioningly keep the Sabbath and all God's commands and thereby enter into God's abode, His dwelling place—His rest.

Chapter 11

It Is Finished

This scripture ("It is finished" John 19:30), is of profound import to us as Christians in understanding many of these passages we have already discussed. What did Christ mean by this? Was He saying that the Ten Commandments were now to be done away with? What was He trying to get across? Come with me in your imagination, as together we travel back to that fateful day some two thousand years ago. Maybe while we are there we can find out His meaning. In the temple, the evening sacrifice is being offered. The priest stands with his knife poised to slay the lamb.

Out on a hill, a short distance from the city, three condemned men suffer the intense agonies of crucifixion. It seems as though the One hanging on the middle cross is carrying the weight of the entire world, and that He cannot endure much longer. Suddenly, in trumpet-like tones that shatter the eerie blackness and send rocks and boulders cascading down the hill, breaking open tombs in their destructive descent toward Jerusalem, the victory cry is heard. "It is finished!" [1]

Back in the temple, all present seem to sense something ominous. The thick, black cloud that surrounded the cross is now hovering low over the city, seeming like the harbinger of doom. The onlookers are unusually quiet and anxious, as if the slightest disturbance, noise or movement might plunge them into judgmental fury. As the priest brings down his hand to slay the innocent victim, a tremendous noise rocks the temple. The people gasp, the knife drops from the priest's suddenly nerveless hand, and the lamb escapes!

All eyes are turned to look at the curtain, ripped by the same hands that wrote doom on the wall of Belshazer's banquet hall. [2] This curtain,

49

Come Ye Yourselves Apart

which has veiled the Shekinah glory, and behind which only the high priest is allowed to go once a year, is now ripped in two, from top to bottom. The former abiding place of God is now open to the view of all. The Holiest of Holies, the mercy seat of God is accessible to all!

Yes! It is finished. The lamb does not need to be offered, because the true Lamb of God has made complete and total atonement for us. No longer is there any need or purpose in the continual offering of lambs, goats, calves or doves! The One to whom they have pointed has come! No longer do we find access to God through the sanctuary, priest or symbols. The curtain is open. All can come freely to God through our Lord and Savior, Jesus Christ.

Unfortunately, most of the Jews did not understand the significance of these events. The curtain was repaired, another lamb was brought and the service continued, without meaning or purpose. While Jesus, the true Lamb and mediator between God and man, was rejected.

It was not the Ten Commandments that Christ declared finished. Oh, no! It was the senseless round of rituals, the endless sacrificing of animals and the heartless worship of the people that was to come to an end. God did not take pleasure in the suffering of His creatures or in the callous worship of his people. Thus it was with triumph that He jubilantly cried, "It is finished!" Yes, praise God! Christ's sacrifice is sufficient to meet the law's demands! It was enough to buy us back from the clutch of Satan. No one needs to be lost. The cost of their redemption has been paid in full!

Chapter 12

Does Faith Make Void the Law?

As we continue to address areas and beliefs that have confused and even misled sincere people, keep in mind that we are here discussing the law of the Ten Commandments. You see, we are often told that the law cannot be obeyed, therefore God's grace must call us righteous when in actuality we are still sinful. We will find the truth as we proceed to talk with Paul and study the life of Jesus.

Paul asked the Romans,

> "Do we then make void the law through faith? God forbid: yea, we establish the law." Romans 3:31

> "...for ye are not under the law but under grace. What then? shall we sin, because we are not under the law, but under grace? God forbid." Romans 6:14,15

> "What shall we say then? Shall we continue in sin, that grace may abound? God forbid. How shall we, that are dead to sin, live any longer therein." Romans 6:1, 2

Obviously, God's grace does not enable us to break His law. What was it that made Christ's death necessary? It was our sin.

> "Who [Jesus] his own self bare our sins in his own body on the tree, that we, being dead to sins, should live unto righteousness: by whose stripes ye were healed." 1 Peter 2:24

But what is sin?

"Whosoever committeth sin transgresseth also the law: for sin is
the transgression of the law." 1 John 3:4

Our breaking or disobeying the law is sin. This disobedience therefore
is the cause of His death. Yet many seem to think that the death designed to
pay the penalty for man's breaking the law in the past was to also give man
the liberty to break the law without penalty in the present. What irony to
think that because the price is paid we are therefore free to go back and do
the very thing that caused His death! Jesus did not die so that the law could
be broken, but because it was broken!

Christ's purpose in coming to earth was to show the entire universe
that the law of God was fair and could be obeyed. In order to do this He
had to come as a human, in human form, and with our fallen nature. It was
in our imperfect nature that He lived a perfect, sinless life. He was tempted
in the same ways that we are, yet He overcame.

"For we have not an high priest which cannot be touched with the
feeling of our infirmities; but was in all points tempted like as we
are, yet without sin." Hebrews 4:15

Now watch closely, because the next verse tells us where He found, and
where we will also find, the power to be over-comers.

"Let us therefore come boldly unto the throne of grace, that
we may obtain mercy, and find grace to help in time of need."
Hebrews 4:16

The Gospels are full of examples of Christ coming boldly before the
throne of grace (see Matthew 14:23; Mark 1:35; 6:46; Luke 5:16; 6:12;
9:18,28). Because He was in continual communion with His Father, He
knew and understood His Father's will. This is the first step in the victorious life, to be in continual communion with our Heavenly Father. In
Luke 22:41-43 we find Christ demonstrating the second step.

Does Faith Make Void the Law?

"And he was withdrawn from them about a stone's cast, and kneeled down, and prayed, Saying, Father, if thou be willing, remove this cup from me: nevertheless not my will, but thine, be done."

Did you see the sequence? First He prays, "remove this cup from Me." This is what He wants, and what His human nature craves. But then He adds, "Not My will but Thine be done." He humbly submits Himself to His loving Father's care. Then notice what happens.

"And there appeared an angel unto him from heaven, strengthening him." Luke 22:41-43

The angel never could have come to Him had He not surrendered His will to His Father, but because He was yielded, the angel came and gave Him the strength that He needed to carry out His Father's will. This is how it will be for us as well. If we refuse to surrender, or even attempt to obey, in our own strength, we will not have Heaven's help. We will be on our own. But when we submit our wills totally to God's, then, although perhaps invisible, angels will attend and give us strength and wisdom to succeed.

Throughout His life, Christ fought and won the victory over every inherited tendency to sin, and now He offers this victory to us. It was by His continual communion with His Father, and an absolute abandonment of self and surrender to the will of God, that made Him victorious. This is the only way we too will find success and victory in our lives. As we through faith lay hold on Christ's victory and continually commune with our Father and surrender to His will, then His victory will become our own. Then in His strength we also will be victorious over sin, as He was.

So often we fail to have victory over the sin in our lives. Why? Because we have attempted to conquer the sin rather than self. You see, Christ has fought and won the battle over every sin. There is no sin that He has left unconquered. It is not for us to battle against sin; that has already been done. The one and only battle that we have to face is with ourselves. Our self-will must die. When self is surrendered we will have nothing but absolute victory over any and all sin. Yes, the law can be obeyed, not out of obligation but as a natural by-product of a continual growing surrender to Him Who has overcome the world—Jesus Christ!

Chapter 13

Faulty Promises

When we talk about law, the Old and New Covenants inevitably come up. To understand the New Covenant we must first understand the Old Covenant. To do this, let us turn to Exodus chapter 19:

'And Moses went up unto God, and the Lord called unto him out of the mountain, saying, Thus shalt thou say to the house of Jacob, and tell the children of Israel; Ye have seen what I did unto the Egyptians, and how I bare you on eagles' wings, and brought you unto myself. Now therefore, *if ye will obey my voice indeed, and keep my covenant, then ye shall be a peculiar treasure unto me above all people: for all the earth is mine: And ye shall be unto me a kingdom of priests, and an holy nation.* These are the words which thou shalt speak unto the children of Israel. And Moses came and called for the elders of the people, and laid before their faces all these words which the Lord commanded him. And all the people answered together, and said, *All that the Lord hath spoken we will do.* And Moses returned the words of the people unto the Lord." Exodus 19:3-8

God promised to bless the people if they would obey. The people heartily covenanted to be obedient. The agreement made on that day, so many years ago, was very much like what we call a Last Will and Testament today. Then, just as now, in order for the covenant to be ratified, there was the necessity of the death. At that time the death of an ox, in type, or representation of Jesus' future sacrifice, was the symbolic ratification of the Old Covenant:

"And Moses came and told the people all the words of the
LORD, and all the judgments: and all the people answered
with one voice, and said, All the words which the LORD
hath said will we do. And Moses wrote all the words of
the LORD, and rose up early in the morning, and builded
an altar under the hill, and twelve pillars, according to
the twelve tribes of Israel. And he sent young men of
the children of Israel, which offered burnt offerings, and
sacrificed peace offerings of oxen unto the LORD. And
Moses took half of the blood, and put it in basons; and
half of the blood he sprinkled on the altar. And he took
the book of the covenant, and read in the audience of the
people: and they said, All that the LORD hath said will
we do, and be obedient. And Moses took the blood, and
sprinkled it on the people, and said, Behold the blood
of the covenant, which the LORD hath made with you
concerning all these words." Exodus 24:3-8

So God presented His law, then made terms with the people. The people agreed to these terms. This was the covenant. The text says that the
covenant was made *concerning* the law. The covenant was not the law itself.
God and the people covenanted regarding the law. If they would obey, God
would bless them abundantly and make them His special treasure.

But we already know what happened, how quickly the people failed.
Paul stresses the point that the failure of the covenant was with the people.
They failed to do their half of the agreement making it impossible for God
to fulfill His half.

"But now hath he obtained a more excellent ministry, by how much
also he is the mediator of a *better covenant*, which was established
upon *better promises*. For if that first covenant had been faultless,
then should no place have been sought for the second. For *finding
fault with them*, he saith, Behold, the days come, saith the Lord,
when I will make a new covenant with the house of Israel and with
the house of Judah: Not according to the covenant that I made
with their fathers in the day when I took them by the hand to lead
them out of the land of Egypt; because *they continued not in my*

covenant, and I regarded them not, saith the Lord. For this is the covenant that I will make with the house of Israel after those days, saith the Lord; **I will put my laws into their mind, and write them in their hearts**: and I will be to them a God, and they shall be to me a people: ... For I will be merciful to their unrighteousness, and their sins and their iniquities will I remember no more." Hebrews 8:6-10, 12 *emphasis supplied*

The fundamental principle for the New Covenant is very much the same as for the Old. The Law is still the basis on which the contract between God and man is made. The only difference is that we lay aside all claim to our own righteousness and depend on God to obey the law in us. God describes this as ingraining His Law in our hearts and minds. In the New Covenant He makes the Law so much a part of our being that obedience becomes as natural as breathing. No longer is it us obeying by grit and determination but by constant surrender to God doing in and through us.

"But," I hear someone say, "The law was done away at the cross. We are not bound to it in these New Testament times." The books of Exodus, Leviticus, and Deuteronomy present many laws covering topics from personal hygiene to civil law. Many of these laws we still observe today, perhaps unwittingly, but because we have learned that they provide the best, safest, healthiest, and happiest modus operandi.

God gave several different laws. There were Civil Laws, Health Laws, Moral Laws, and Ceremonial Laws. The first three of these are practical laws upon which the happiness of all society is dependant. What condition would we be in if we allowed thieves or murderers immunity? We can see the tragedy of the failure to observe God's Laws for fullest health in the sad consequences of Egyptian diseases, like cancer, heart disease, and diabetes rampaging our society (Deuteronomy 7:12, 15; Exodus 15:26). The Moral, Civil, and Health Laws are God's laws for us today just as they were for all mankind prior to the cross.

But what about Paul's clear declaration to the Colossians that the law is nailed to the cross? We discuss these verses more in their own chapter but here we will take a quick glance.

"Blotting out the handwriting of ordinances that was against us, which was contrary to us, and took it out of the way, nailing it to

Come Ye Yourselves Apart

his cross; ... Let no man therefore judge you in [things] ... Which are a shadow of things to come. ..." Colossians 2:14, 17

The key phrase we will look at here is "shadow of things to come." Does the Moral Law typify anything regarding the Messiah? Thou shalt not make unto thee any graven image (Ex. 20:4-6)? Or Thou shalt not take the name of the Lord in vain (Ex. 20:7)? There is nothing symbolic there. What about the Health Law? Is there any Messianic symbolism to the command to abstain from eating blood, fat, things strangled and creatures declared unclean (Leviticus 11 & Deuteronomy)? None. Although science is demonstrating that there are very strong health reasons. Or the Civil Law, is it symbolic? Pay a just wage to all servants (Deuteronomy 24:14,15) or measure with honest weights (Deuteronomy 25:13-16)? Of course not.

How about the Ceremonial Law? The lamb without blemish, the blood poured on the ground at the base of the alter, are poignant symbols of Jesus' perfection and the spilling of His blood at the foot of the cross. In every facet and nuance the ceremonial law was clearly a foreshadowing of Jesus and His ministry on earth and in heaven following His ascension (see Hebrews 8:4,5; 9:9-14; 10:8-10).

The Ceremonial Laws surrounding the Sanctuary system, were the shadows, figures, and types that were met in Jesus. As they met their fulfillment in Him, they were discontinued. It is like a child who has gone off to war. The family cherishes pictures and letters but suppose how silly it would be if, when the child returns, the family runs to the pictures and cries and holds them. It is the same with the Sanctuary system. It was a picture of Jesus and His ministry in our behalf. But now that He has come, why would we want to embrace the picture instead of Him? While it is important to understand the Sanctuary and its imagery from a prophetic view, there is no reason for its active continuance.

"It was therefore necessary that the *patterns* of things in the heavens should be purified with these (animal sacrifices); but the heavenly things themselves with better sacrifices. For Christ is not entered into the holy places made with [human] hands, which are *figures* of the true; but into heaven itself, now to appear in the presence of God for us: ... So Christ was once offered to bear the sins of many;

Faulty Promises

and unto them that look for him shall he appear the second time without sin unto salvation." Hebrews 9:23, 24, 28

So while the picture or drama, if you will, of Jesus' ministry for us is no longer effectual today, God's eternal government still operates on God's everlasting moral law.

So where was the failure? What is and why is there a New Covenant? Paul leaves us no question as to where the problem lies:

"For what the law could not do, in that it was weak through *the flesh*, God sending his own Son in the likeness of sinful flesh, and for sin, condemned sin in the flesh: That the righteousness of the law might be fulfilled in us, who walk *not* after the flesh, but after the Spirit." Romans 8:3, 4

The problem was us! We attempted to obey through our own strength and will. We were incorrigibly unregenerate, determined to rebel. Even our attempts to obey were actuated by evil impulses. Did God intentionally make it impossible for us? Not at all. His power was as available to Cain as it was to Abel, as accessible to the Congregation of Israel as to Moses. Where was the problem then? The problem was and always has been with the covenant *concerning* the Law. Man's maxim has almost without exception been "All that the Lord hath spoken *we will do*" (Exodus 19:8). This was where the Law was weak—in our flesh, in us.

Chapter 14

Abraham and the Covenants

Paul gives us the analogy of Abraham and his two wives as representing the two Covenants. Sarah represented the New Covenant because Abraham trusted and depended entirely on God to have a child with her. His obedience was an evidence of his trust, reliance, and dependency on God. Hagar, on the other hand, was a type of the Old Covenant. Abraham trusted himself, his own ability. His disobedience showed his dependence on human conniving, human strength. Paul tells us,

"For it is written, that Abraham had two sons, the one by a bondmaid, the other by a freewoman. Now we, brethren, as Isaac was, are the children of promise." Galatians 4:22, 28

The bondwoman was Abraham's attempt to 'help God out of a corner.' At the start Abraham and Sarah did not believe God was big enough to fulfill His promise. They did not trust His word. They were in bondage to distrust, anxiety, worry, fear, and guilt. Abraham was outside of the will of God, depending on himself. He was enslaved. Abraham was trying to act on what God had said, but he was attempting to do it in his own strength with his own finite wisdom. This is the Old Covenant experience. Attempting to obey God all on our own. We always fail and we always make things worse and ourselves more miserable. In the end, we are farther from our goal than when we started, and we create a lot of unhappiness along the way.

Thankfully, there is a freewoman in Abraham's experience. Abraham learned to cast all his weight on God's promises, to trust Him only and to leave the fulfillment of God's will in His hands. God did not fail him either. He worked a miracle. Free from worry, fear, and guilt, Abraham and Sarah were truly free and happy in faithful obedience because it was God working in them. This is the New Covenant life.

Just as God brought physical life out of the dead womb of Sarah so He brings the person dead in sin and guilt, in bondage to sin's condemnation, into abundant life, free from all of sin's entanglements. No longer is he constantly striving vainly to do right, his heart is changed, and God is doing in him what he could never do on his own. He takes hold of God's strength, trusts fully on Him and thereby he finds victory and life.

The New Covenant is surrendering all our heart and all our known choices to God. Then God can do in our spiritually dead bodies what he did for Sarah. He will create a miraculous, obedient life in place of our dead one. The New Covenant is implicit trust and dependence on God, on His working in us, "both to will and to do of His good pleasure." (Philippians 2:13)

The Old Covenant is indeed a miserable existence at best, **not** because of the Law, but because we are looking to ourselves for the ability to obey. The New Covenant is a joyous life because it is lived through the power of Jesus in habitual obedience to God's requirements of love. Jesus said,

> "Whosoever committeth sin is the servant of sin. ... If the Son therefore shall make you free, ye shall be free indeed." John 8:34-36

The Old Covenant was only faulty in that humans were attempting through human power to overcome the demonic powers of Satan's temptations. What impossible, fool-hearty presumption! Freedom is only in Jesus. In Him we find the forgiveness for our past and infinite power over Satan's wiles for the present!

Were those living in Old Testament times saved through the Old Testament Covenant of works while we are saved under the New Testament Covenant of faith? The answer is no. In both the Old and New Testaments we find examples of people choosing to live under both Covenants. Remember Abraham? Only those who have a New Covenant experience as he did can be saved. God tells us that the Covenant He longs to make with us today has always been available:

> "Now the God of peace, that brought again from the dead our Lord Jesus, that great shepherd of the sheep, through the blood of

the *everlasting covenant*, Make you perfect in every good work to do his will, working in you that which is wellpleasing in his sight, through Jesus Christ; to whom be glory for ever and ever. Amen." Hebrews 13:20-21 (emphasis supplied)

You see, the everlasting, New Covenant is God working in us, doing His will. The Old Covenant is really an experience of rebellion. Sadly, the keeping of Sunday is the Old Covenant attempt of obeying God in our own wisdom. But we do not need to stay under the Old Covenant. Like Abraham we can put away the bondage and find the freedom of New Covenant obedience. Through implicit faith in Jesus, we can keep God's Sabbath, the only true Sabbath, at His specified time and in His way. We *can* experience the New Covenant walk with God.

Chapter 15

Sunday and the New Covenant

In the Bible, the words "Testament" and "Covenant" are used interchangeably as we will see in the next few passages. Since a Covenant in Bible times was like our Last Will and Testament today, there needed to be a death for it to be ratified. It could not be effective until the death of the "testator."

> "For where a testament is, there must also of necessity be the death of the testator. For a testament is of force after men are dead: otherwise it is of no strength at all while the testator liveth." Hebrews 9:16, 17

In the Old Testament an ox was slain as ratification of the Old Covenant in type of Jesus' future death. In the New Testament, the New Covenant also had to be ratified by the shedding of blood. This time it was not a typical or symbolic sacrifice of an ox but the antitypical, actual sacrifice of the Son of God. Jesus spoke of this ratification of the New Covenant in the Upper Room just before His death:

> "And as they were eating, Jesus took bread, and blessed it, and brake it, and gave it to the disciples, and said, Take, eat; this is my body. And he took the cup, and gave thanks, and gave it to them, saying, Drink ye all of it; For this is my blood of the *new testament*, which is shed for many for the remission of sins." Matthew 26:26-28

Come Ye Yourselves Apart

Here Christ instituted the last supper. The juice was a figure of His blood soon to be shed for the ratification of the New Covenant. Have you ever wondered why He instituted the communion service at that time? The disciples did not even understand what He was talking about—shedding His blood? They were looking for Him to establish an earthly, conquering kingdom. Why didn't He wait until after His resurrection to set up this memorial of His death? Why do it before they could understand?

This special service of remembrance was to continue until Jesus' second coming.

"For as often as ye eat this bread, and drink this cup, ye do shew the Lord's death till he come." 1 Corinthians 11:26

As such it needed to be a part of the New Testament or the New Covenant. Whatever was to be instituted as a part of the New Covenant had to be added before the Covenant was ratified, before Jesus' death. No more additions or changes could be made after the Covenant was ratified, after His death. Jesus had to introduce the Last Supper before His death in order for it to become a part of the New Covenant. His death would ratify, or as Paul says, "confirm" the Testament and nothing more could be added or taken out.

"Brethren, I speak after the manner of men; Though it be but a man's covenant, yet if it be confirmed, no man disannulleth, or addeth thereto." Galatians 3:15

This point is critical to our discussion of Sunday sacredness. Protestantism tells us that the reason for keeping Sunday is that we are under the New Covenant and that Sunday is a memorial of Christ's resurrection. But there is a hitch. When did the observance of Sunday begin? We have already seen that it was not officially commanded of Christians until 336 AD, several centuries after Jesus' death.

But for our discussion here, suppose the disciples did begin worshiping on that very first Resurrection Sunday—just two days after Christ's death. It would have been two days too late. The Covenant had already been ratified the Friday evening before. Even just a few days later is too late to add or change anything. For Sunday to be part of the New Covenant,

66

Sunday and the New Covenant

Jesus had to institute it previous to His death. But He did not, not even by implication. Sunday is not and never could be a part of the New Covenant since it came after the cross.

Chapter 16

Forthright Admissions

Many of today's churches admit that, indeed, only Saturday is the true Sabbath. Let us take a look at just a few of the statements they have made.

Anglican

"Where are we told in Scripture that we are to keep the first day at all? We are commanded to keep the seventh; but we are nowhere commanded to keep the first day." Isaac Williams, D.D., *Plain Sermons on the Catechism*, Volume 1, p. 334. [1]

"We have made the change from the seventh day to the first day, from Saturday to Sunday, on the authority of one holy Catholic Church." Bishop Seymour, *Why We Keep Sunday*, Article 12. [1]

Baptist

"We believe that the Law of God is the eternal and imperishable rule of His moral government." *Baptist Church Manual.* [1]

"We will now...show that the sanctification of the Sabbath has its foundation and its origin in a law which God at creation itself established for the whole world, and as a consequence therefore is binding on all men in all ages." *Evangelisten, (The Evangelist)*, Stockholm, May 30 to August 15, 1863 (organ of the Swedish Baptist Church). [2]

Come Ye Yourselves Apart

"There was and is a commandment to keep holy the Sabbath day, but that Sabbath day was not Sunday. ... It will be said, however, and with some show of triumph, that the Sabbath was transferred from the seventh to the first day of the week. ... Where can the record of such a transaction be found? Not in the New Testament—absolutely not. There is no scriptural evidence of the change of the Sabbath institution from the seventh to the first day of the week." Dr. Edward T. Hiscox, author of *The Baptist Manual*, in a paper read at the New York Ministers' Conference, November 13,1893. [1]

"The Sabbath was established originally in no special connection with the Hebrews, but as an institution for all mankind, in commemoration of God's rest after six days of creation. It was designed for all the descendants of Adam." Southern Baptist Convention series adult quarterly, August 15, 1937. [1]

Congregationalist

"The current notion that Christ and His apostles authoritatively substituted the first day for the seventh is absolutely without authority in the New Testament." Dr. Lyman Abbott, *Christian Union*, Jan. 19, 1882. [1]

Lutheran

"...Scripture has in no way ordained the first day of the week in place of the Sabbath. There is simply no law in the New Testament to that effect." John T. Mueller, *Sabbath or Sunday?* p. 16. [1]

"God blessed the Sabbath and sanctified it to Himself. God willed that this command concerning the Sabbath should remain. He willed that on the seventh day the word should be preached." Dr. Martin Luther, *Commentary on Genesis*, Volume 1, p. 138-140. [2]

"They [Catholics] allege the Sabbath changed into Sunday, the Lord's day, contrary to the decalogue, as it appears, neither is there any example more boasted of than the changing of the Sabbath

Forthright Admissions

day." Martin Luther, *Augsburg Confession of Faith*, Article 28, par. 9. [1]

"I wonder exceedingly how it came to be imputed to me that I should reject the law of Ten Commandments. ... Whosoever abrogates the law must of necessity abrogate sin also." Martin Luther, *Spiritual Antichrist*, p. 71, 72. [1]

Methodist

"This 'handwriting of ordinances' our Lord did blot out, take away, and nail to His cross. (Colossians 2:14.) But the moral law contained in the Ten Commandments, and enforced by the prophets, He did not take away. ... The moral law stands on an entirely different foundation from the ceremonial or ritual law. ... Every part of this law must remain in force upon all mankind and in all ages." John Wesley, *Sermons on Several Occasions,* 2 Volume Edition, Volume 1, p. 221, 222. [1]

"The Sabbath was made for MAN; not for the Hebrews, but for all men." E. O. Haven, *Pillars of Truth,* p. 88. [1]

Moody Bible Institute

"When Christ was on earth He did nothing to set it [the Sabbath] aside; He freed it from the traces under which the scribes and Pharisees had put it, and gave it its true place. 'The Sabbath was made for man, and not man for the Sabbath.' It is just as practicable and as necessary for men today as it ever was—in fact, more than ever, because we live in such an intense age." Dwight L. Moody, *Weighed and Wanting,* p. 46. [1]

"The Sabbath was binding in Eden, and it has been in force ever since. The fourth commandment begins with the word 'remember,' showing that the Sabbath already existed when God wrote the law on the tables of stone at Sinai. How can men claim that this one commandment has been done away when they will admit that the other nine are still binding?" ibid, p. 47. [1]

Roman Catholic

"The Adventists are the only body of Christians with the Bible as their teacher, ... Hence their appellation, 'Seventh-day Adventists.' Their cardinal principle consists in setting apart Saturday for the exclusive worship of God, in conformity with the positive command of God Himself, repeatedly reiterated in the sacred books of the Old and New Testaments, literally obeyed by the Children of Israel for thousands of years to this day, and indorsed by the teaching and practice of the Son of God whilst on earth.

"Per contra, the Protestants of the world, the Adventists excepted, with the *same* Bible as their cherished and sole infallible teacher, by their practice, since their appearance in the sixteenth century,... have rejected the day named for His worship by God, and assumed, in apparent contradiction of His command, a day for His worship never once referred to for that purpose, in the pages of that Sacred Volume." *Catholic Mirror*, September 2, 1893. [3]

"The Protestant world has been, from its infancy, in the sixteenth century, in thorough accord with the Catholic Church, in keeping 'holy', not Saturday, but Sunday ... appealing to their common teacher, the Bible, the great body of Protestants, ... have no other resource left than the admission that they have been teaching and practicing *what is Scripturally false for over three centuries,* by adopting the teaching and practice of what they have always pretended to believe an apostate church, contrary to every warrant and teaching of sacred Scripture." Ibid. [3]

"It was upon this very point that the Reformation was condemned by the Council of Trent. The Reformers had constantly charged, as here stated, that the Catholic Church had apostatized from the truth *as contained in the written word.* 'The written word', 'The Bible and the Bible only',...this was the proclaimed platform of the Reformation and of Protestantism. 'The scripture *and tradition,*' 'The Bible as interpreted by the Church'...this was the position and claim of the Catholic Church. This was the main issue in the

Forthright Admissions

Council of Trent, ... The question was debated day after day until the council was fairly brought to a standstill. Finally, after a long and intense mental strain, the Archbishop of Reggio came into the council with substantially the following argument...

"'The Protestants claim to stand upon the written word only. They profess to hold the Scripture alone as the standard of faith. They justify their revolt by the plea that the Church has apostatized from the written word and follows tradition. Now the Protestants' claim that they stand on the written word only is not true. Their profession of holding the Scripture alone as the standard of faith is false. Proof: The written word explicitly enjoins the observance of the seventh day as the Sabbath. They do not observe the seventh day, but reject it. If they do truly hold the Scripture alone as their standard, they would be observing the seventh day as is enjoined in the Scripture throughout. Yet they not only reject the observance of the Sabbath enjoined in the written word, but they have adopted and do practice the observance of Sunday, for which they have only the tradition of the Church. ...' (See the proceedings of the Council; Augsburg Confession; and Encyclopedia Britannica article: Trent, Council of)." *Rome's Challenge*, p. 25-27. [3]

Presbyterian

"The Sabbath is part of the decalogue—the Ten Commandments. This alone forever settles the question as to the perpetuity of the institution. ... Until therefore it can be shown that the whole moral law has been repealed, the Sabbath will stand. ... The teaching of Christ confirms the perpetuity of the Sabbath." T. C. Blake, D. D., *Theology Condensed*, p. 474, 475. [1]

"We must not imagine that the coming of Christ has freed us from the authority of the law; for it is the eternal rule of a devout and holy life, and must therefore be as unchangeable as the justice of God, ...is constant and uniform." John Calvin, *Commentary on a Harmony of the Gospels*, Volume 1, p. 277. [1]

Come Ye Yourselves Apart

Objective Researcher of Various Religions

"In Acts 20:7 we read that 'upon the first day of the week, when the disciples came together to break bread, Paul preached unto them.' However, this doesn't say that the Sabbath should be shifted from Saturday to Sunday, any more than the common habit of a Wednesday night prayer meeting or Bible study makes Wednesday the new day of rest and worship.

"... if one looks solely for biblical evidence, the theological argument is probably stronger for maintaining Saturday as the day of rest. Throughout mainstream Christianity, then, a major change rests more on tradition than on Scripture." *The New Believers,* David V. Barrett, p. 126. [4]

Chapter 17

A Glance at the Imminent Future

Where dose all this lead? Does the Sabbath carry some cataclysmic implications for everyone in the not-so-distant future? Indeed it does! The Bible tells us that a religio-political super power will govern all nations. This power will enact laws that will demand all people, in all countries, to keep Sunday sacred or be killed. This is when no one will escape. All must decide who they will serve.

Just as God's seal, the Sabbath, shows that we are His when we keep it out of love for Him, so the keeping of Sunday will show that we are not God's, but instead opposed to His government.

The mark of opposition to God can be received in either the head or in the hand. Receiving the mark in the forehead means that all who accept it at that time will knowingly make a conscience choice to disobey God by willingly keeping Sunday as sacred. To receive the mark in one's hand means that the person knows what is right but, rather than endanger his personal safety, tries to serve God undercover. He therefore futilely attempts to obey God at heart, stifling the dictates of his own conscience while outwardly conforming to the dictates of man by keeping the counterfeit Sabbath.

In contrast, God's seal can only be received in the forehead because the Sabbath must be so much a part of every fiber of our being that we could not condone Sunday sacredness even by implication through our actions or words. The Sabbath must be so ingrained in the heart and in the life that it would be easier for us to die than to trample on the Sabbath or any of God's fair and loving laws.

Just as the test for the three faithful Hebrews (Daniel 3) was about who they would worship—God or the golden statue, an institution of man—so it will be for us. Who will we choose to worship? As Nebuchadnezzar's

75

Come Ye Yourselves Apart

decree extended to all peoples, tongues, tribes and nations, and was enforced at the cost of life itself, so it will shortly be for us as well.

God will have a people who will be faithful to Him, though the price will be great. Yet just as was the case with the three faithful Hebrews, God will be with those who must walk through the fire. He has promised:

> "... Fear not: for I have redeemed thee, I have called thee by thy name; thou art mine. When thou passest through the waters, I will be with thee; and through the rivers, they shall not overflow thee: when thou walkest through the fire, thou shalt not be burned; neither shall the flame kindle upon thee. For I am the LORD thy God...thy Saviour...Fear not: for I am with thee...Ye are my witnesses, saith the LORD, and my servant whom I have chosen..." Isaiah 43:1-3, 5, 10.

Jesus is gently calling to you. Have you heard His voice? He says, "I know the path is not easy, for I have walked it too. I know the cup is bitter, but I have tasted its bitterness for you. The cross is heavy, but I will take its heaviness for you if you will follow Me." He tenderly says, "Come, My child, I cannot bear to not have you with Me where I am. I have paid the price. The gift is yours; the mansions in Heaven are for you, so please do not turn away. Heaven is not Heaven if My loved ones are not there." Will you accept Christ's invitation? He is calling to you, dear child of His. What will your answer be?

Chapter 18

Keeping the Sabbath Holy

Now that we know what the Sabbath is, how can we keep it holy? Has God set perimeters around His holy day? Let us see if we can find the answer to that in God's Word.

The Sabbath is a sacred 24-hour period during which we and God can communicate more personally and know each other intimately. No long-lasting, meaningful relationship can exist if the two individuals do not spend personal, undistracted time together. This is exactly what Satan is trying to prevent. He is making determined efforts to keep us so busy that we will not have this time to spend with our Lord. He knows that if we do spend this time with God we will not so easily fall for his temptations. God wants to individually give us Himself, but Satan is seeking to keep us away so that we will miss out on the greatest blessings that God longs to give us. So far, Satan has run a very successful scheme, but he doesn't need to be so successful in preventing you and me from receiving God's fullest blessings.

There are things that God has said will enhance our day with Him, and other things that will hinder our relationship or take our time away from Him. Let us take a look at these things.

When Does the Sabbath Begin?

In telling the Children of Israel how to keep the Day of Atonement (a ceremonial Sabbath), God said:

"...in the ninth day of the month at even, from even unto even, shall ye celebrate your sabbath" Leviticus 23:32.

In Deuteronomy we are told what "even" means:

"... at even, at the going down of the sun. ..." Deuteronomy 16:6

And in Nehemiah 13:19 we are told that the seventh-day Sabbath was also kept in this way.

"And it came to pass, that when the gates of Jerusalem began to be dark before the sabbath, I commanded that the gate should be shut, and charged that they should not be opened till after the sabbath. ..."

The Sabbath was still kept this way when Christ came.

"And [Jesus and His disciples] went into Capernaum; and straightway on the sabbath day he entered into the synagogue, and taught. ... And at even, when the sun did set, they brought unto him all that were diseased. ..." Mark 1:21, 32

It must be realized that the religious leaders in Israel had distorted the meaning of "rest" and would not allow much to be done on the Sabbath. Even bringing emotional, mental or physical relief to the suffering was considered a sin. This is *not* how Jesus intended the Sabbath to kept. After giving an example of relieving the needs of an animal, He said:

"...Wherefore it is lawful to do well on the sabbath days." Matthew 12:12

Jesus considered healing on the Sabbath consistent with His Father's loving law. He often healed on the Sabbath, in fact. But when the Pharisees could, they did not let the people come to Him for healing during the Sabbath hours. Mark 1:32 does illustrate, however, that the Sabbath still began and ended in the New Testament as it had in the Old. It began Friday evening when the sun went down and lasted until Saturday evening at sunset—"from even to even."

Keeping the Sabbath Holy

Food Preparation for the Sabbath

In Exodus, God admonished His people to prepare as much of the food as possible ahead of time so that they would have more worry-free time to spend with Him. This is still applicable to us today, especially since we have conveniences that allow us to keep prepared food fresh for longer periods of time than they could.

> "And he said unto them, This is that which the LORD hath said, To morrow is the rest of the holy sabbath unto the LORD: bake that which ye will bake to day, and seethe [boil] that ye will seethe. ..."
> Exodus 16:23

You will also remember how Israel was to collect extra manna on Friday because God would not send them any on the Sabbath. He wants us to be able to give our full attention to Him. This can be done in a more complete way when we are prepared as much as possible ahead of time with everything, not just food.

General Guiding Principles

There are certain jobs that are unavoidable and must be done every day.* Both people and animals need their physical and emotional needs cared for. But as much as can be done ahead of time should be, or left un-done until after sundown. Regular workday jobs should be put away, both physically and mentally, during the Sabbath.

NOTE:

Certain jobs that are unavoidable are, for example: nursing, emergency healthcare and animal care in general. Animals must be fed and watered, some milked, and any injuries cared for. It would be wrong for these things to be neglected, because we would be causing emotional, physical or mental pain or discomfort to God's creatures, whether human or animal.

It is good to help relieve the emotional or physical burdens, and this is what Christ was often doing (see Luke 13:14-17; John 5:1-18). The day can also be spent in fellowship with fellow believers sharing a meal, going for a nature walk, sharing testimonies or the previous week's blessings, favorite verses, and new spiritual insights learned. The list goes on and on.

Come Ye Yourselves Apart

It is important, though, that while we guard the Sabbath hours we do not become caught up with the "do's and don'ts." Instead, use these two little questions to determine what you will and will not do.

#1. Will this activity draw me closer to Jesus?

#2. Is this activity necessary?

There are times when something will neither take your attention away from Jesus or bring it to Him. In these cases, question # 2 can have the final say.

Chapter 19

The Sabbath in a Nutshell

God has given us so much; there is no reason for us to misunderstand His will for us. Let us briefly summarize what we have studied.

Where the Sabbath Began

The Sabbath began in the Garden of Eden (see Genesis 2:3). It, along with marriage, was the only thing that Adam and Eve brought out of the Garden of Eden after their fall. It was a day that they had spent one on one with Jesus in the garden. What an awesome way to spend the Sabbath!

Israel and the Sabbath

At Mount Sinai, God reiterated to the Jews the sacredness of the Sabbath (see Exodus 20:8-11). God had to refresh the Israelites' memory because they had been in a heathen nation for so long that they had nearly forgotten the precepts of God, which their grandparents had followed. This is why God begins the fourth commandment with "Remember." They were already aware of its sacredness.

God knew how easy it would be for future generations to forget the Sabbath. As society became more and more technical, and life became faster paced, He also knew how important a day of rest with Himself would be. This is why He says "Remember" to us as well! It is also interesting and yet ironic how the very day that God made a special point of telling us to remember is the very day that most are telling us to forget!

The Sabbath When Jesus Came

When Christ came, the Sabbath had become a burden because the religious leaders taught that a person must keep as many rules as possible. And when they ran out of rules they invented more. They thought that the rules would save them instead of accepting the One Who gave the original simple and loving laws. They replaced *being* Christ's, with *doing for* Him.

When Jesus came He showed through His life how He and the Father had intended for the Sabbath to be kept (see Mark 1:21; Luke 4:16; and Luke 6:6). Even in death, Christ kept the Sabbath sacred. He did all that needed to be done in the sacrificial phase of saving man before the sun set, before the Sabbath had begun. He rested peacefully in the grave through the Sabbath hours. Then He arose early Sunday, soon to begin the mediatorial phase of saving man (see Luke 23:53, 54, 56; Luke 24:1-3).

Did the Disciples Observe the Sabbath?

We find in the book of Acts that even after Christ's death and resurrection, the disciples continued to keep the Sabbath holy, revealing that Jesus had never said anything to them about the Sabbath being changed. They kept the Sabbath themselves and also taught those in the Gentile churches to do the same (see Acts 13:14, 42, 44; 16:13; 17:2; 18:4). Either Christ's disciples were boldly disobeying, or they were unaware of any transfer of solemnity from Saturday to Sunday.

Which Day Is the Lord's?

Exodus 20:10, Isaiah 58:13, Matthew 12:8 and Luke 6:5 all say that the seventh-day Sabbath is the day of the Lord; thus, the Lord's Day that John refers to in Revelation 1:10 is the Sabbath. In fact, worship on Sunday was not introduced into the Christian world until over 200 years after Revelation was written! It cannot then be claimed that Sunday was commonly called the "Lord's Day" at that time. Neither can it be claimed that Sunday worship is what John was talking about, since he never saw Christian Sunday worship in his lifetime. When he *later* wrote the gospel of John, he still regarded the seventh day as the only Sabbath (John 5:9, 10, 16, 18; 7:22, 23; 9:14, 16; 19:31).

The Sabbath Lived On

A careful historical study of the Sabbath will reveal that throughout the centuries, from the time of the disciples until today, there has always been a people that were faithful and who reverenced the seventh day as the Sabbath. Many of the Christian churches of Pella, Palestine, all the way to India, Italy, China, Scotland, Ireland, Persia, France, the British Isles, Bohemia, Wales and America sanctified the seventh day. Those Sabbath-keeping Christian church groups included Celts, Abyssinians, Jacobites, Marinites, Armenians, Nestorians, Paulicians, Petrobusians, Passaginians, Waldenses, Insabbatati and the Taipings.

Who Changed The Sabbath?

Both history and their own writings reveal that the Roman Church (or Catholic Church) made the change of sanctity from Saturday to Sunday. In fact, she proudly boasts of making the change. And the Protestant world, which claims to obey the Bible and the Bible only, and who so unsparingly condemns Rome's practice of tradition, humbly submits to following her sabbath on Sunday, which has no hint of authority in the Word of God, the Bible.

The Seal of God and the Mark of the Beast

The seventh-day Sabbath will be God's seal (see Exodus 31:17; Ezekiel 20:11, 12, 19, 20). In the last days, just before His return, this seal will show who are and are not God's true people. The opposing power also has a mark (see Revelation 13:16; 14:9-12) and is more than willing to openly claim as its mark the worship of a false sabbath, which is Sunday.

The True Memorial of the Resurrection

Since Sunday is not a memorial of Christ's resurrection, what is? Surely God would want us to remember something as important as the resurrection of His Son. Wouldn't He leave something for us so we would not forget? Yes, and that is what He did by leaving us the ordinance of baptism. Jesus was baptized by immersion (see Mark 1:9, 10). The disciples also baptized people using the method of immersion (see Acts 8:36, 38, 39). Baptism by immersion is a perfect memorial for the death, burial and resurrection of Jesus (see Colossians 2:12; Romans 6:3, 4).

The foot washing and communion service is another memorial and commemoration of the same event.

The Law, Is it Still Valid?

The law is God's character in written form, thus it cannot be changed or abolished without changing or abolishing God. The law is as enduring as its Author. The reason for obeying the law should not be simply to keep from sinning, but because we love God and *want* to obey Him. If the Ten Commandments could have been changed, then Christ would not have needed to come to earth and pay the penalty that the law demands for its transgression.

The very fact that He came and died is evidence of the law's validity and continuance, not its abolishment (Matthew 5:17, 18)! Isaiah 66:23 says that the Sabbath will be kept in Heaven and on the New Earth, which shows that it could not have been done away with at the cross, because we will still be keeping it in Heaven—forever!

It Is Finished!

When Christ cried, "It is finished" from the cross, was He saying that the Ten Commandments were done away with? No. But what *was* finished? Oh, the joy of every Christian; the symbolism and ceremonies were done away! Now we have personal access to God through Jesus Christ, who rent the curtain that stood between us. He, the perfect Lamb, needed only to be offered once. His

The Sabbath in a Nutshell

blood is powerful enough to forgive every single sin of every single individual that ever lived or would live. No more need of the continual bloodshed of countless innocent lambs, calves and goats. Yes, the entire ceremonial system has been done away, and it is no longer the way to God. *Jesus,* the one to whom all these things pointed, has come. Therefore, the symbols are no longer needed. We can come boldly to the throne of grace, because Jesus, our Brother, is there pleading for our cause (see Hebrews 4:16).

Faith and the Law

Many make the claim that faith and God's grace make the law void, but is this true? Both Paul and James dealt with the same question in their day, and their answers are still applicable for our eternal benefit today (see Romans 3:31; 6:1, 2, 14, 15; James 1:22-25; 2:19-24). Through His life, Jesus gave beautiful examples by how He lived and how we also can live in perfect obedience to His and our Heavenly Father's will. He was in continual communion with God (see Matthew 14:23; Mark 1:35; 6:46; Luke 5:16; 6:12; 9:18, 28). He was also surrendered to His Father's will, and because of that Heaven was able to attend, strengthen and give Him wisdom (see Luke 22:41-43).

The New Covenant

The Old Covenant was man promising to obey God's law in his own strength (Exodus 24:3). Man promptly failed at this (see Exodus 32:1-6). Thus a New Covenant was needed, based on that same loving law, but this time written on man's heart (see Jeremiah 31:31-33; Romans 8:3, 4; Hebrews 8:10). When the law of God is written in the heart, it becomes a delight to obey rather than an obligation.

How Is the Sabbath to Be Kept?

Leviticus 23:32, Nehemiah 13:19, and Mark 1:21, 32 tell us that the day is figured from evening to evening and that the Sabbath is to be kept holy during these hours. Exodus 16:23 says that food preparation should be done as much as possible before the Sabbath

Come Ye Yourselves Apart

begins. While some types of work cannot be avoided, whatever is not necessary should be left undone (see Jeremiah 17:22).

The Sabbath is a day to bring relief and comfort to those about us (see Matthew 12:12; Luke 13:14-17; and John 5:1-8). It is a day to spend with like believers, ministering spiritually to others or out in God's creation (see Luke 4:16; Acts 16:13). There are two simple questions that can help us determine if an activity is appropriate for the Sabbath.

#1: Will this activity draw me closer to Jesus?

#2: Is it necessary?

The Sabbath is a special day for us to rest from our works, and this enables God to work in us.

Appendix

The Sabbath Through the Centuries

First Century A.D.

"Then the spiritual seed of Abraham [Christians] fled to Pella, on the other side of Jordan, where they found a safe place of refuge, and could serve their Master and keep His Sabbath." *Eusebius's Ecclesiastical History* Book 3, chapter 5. [1]

Philo, the philosopher and historian, also affirms that this Sabbath was on the seventh day of the week, and was observed universally. *Notes and Queries,* Volume 4, p. 99. [1]

Second Century A.D.

"The primitive Christians had a great veneration for the Sabbath, and spent the day in devotion and sermons. ... They derived this practice from the apostles themselves, as appears by several scriptures to that purpose." D. T. H. Morer, Church of England, *Dialogues on the Lord's Day,* p. 189. [1]

"...The Sabbath was a strong tie which united them with the life of the whole people, and in keeping the Sabbath holy they followed not only the example but the command of Jesus." *Geschichte des Sonntags,* p. 13, 14. [1]

"The Gentile Christians observed also the Sabbath." *Gieseler's Church History*, Volume 1, chapter 2, paragraph 30, 93. [1]

Third Century A.D.

"Thou shalt observe the Sabbath, on account of him who ceased from His work of Creation, but ceased not from his work of Providence: it is a rest for meditation of the law, not for idleness of the hands." *The Anti-Nicene Fathers*, Volume 7, p. 413. From *Constitutions of the Holy Apostles*, a document of the third and fourth centuries. [1]

Fourth Century A.D.

"The ancient Christians were very careful in the observation of Saturday, or the seventh day...It is plain that all the Oriental Churches, and the greatest part of the world, observed the Sabbath as a festival...Athanasius likewise tells us that they held religious assembles on the Sabbath, not because they were infected with Judaism, but to worship Jesus the Lord of the Sabbath, Epiphanius says the same." *Antiquities of the Christian Church*, Volume II, book XX, chapter 3, section 1, 66.1137,1138. [1]

Fifth Century A.D.

"In 411 [Mingana, leader of the Eastern Churches] appointed a metropolitan director for China. These churches were sanctifying the seventh day." J.F. Coltheart, *The Sabbath Through the Centuries*, p. 11. [1]

Sixth Century A.D.

"In this latter instance they [the Scottish church] seem to have followed a custom of which we find traces in the early monastic church of Ireland by which they held Saturday to be the Sabbath on which they rested from all their labors." W.T. Skene, *Adamnan's Life of St. Columba*, 1874, p. 96. [1]

Appendix

Seventh Century A.D.

"It seems to have been customary in the Celtic churches of early times, in Ireland as well as Scotland, to keep Saturday…as a day of rest from labor. They obeyed the fourth commandment literally on the seventh day of the week." James C. Moffatt D.D., professor of Church History at Princeton, *The Church in Scotland*, p. 140. [1]

Eighth Century A.D.

In India, China, Persia, etc., "Widespread and enduring was the observance of the seventh-day Sabbath among the believers of the Church of the East and the Saint Thomas Christians of India, who never were connected with Rome. It was also maintained among those bodies which broke off from Rome after the council of Chalcedon, namely the Abyssinians, the Jacobites, the Marionites and the Armenians." *New Schaff Herzog Encyclopedia of Religious Knowledge*, article, "Nestorians." [2]

Ninth Century A.D.

"Pope Nicholas I, in the ninth century, sent the ruling prince of Bulgaria a long document saying in it that one is to cease from work on Sunday, but not on the Sabbath. The head of the Greek Church, offended at the interference of the Papacy, declared the Pope excommunicated." B.G. Wilkinson, Ph.D., *Truth Triumphant*, p. 232. [2]

Tenth Century A.D.

"The Nestorians eat no pork and keep the Sabbath. They believe neither in auricular confession nor purgatory." *New Schaff Herzog Encyclopedia*, article "Nestorians." [2]

The Waldenses, of apostolic decent, also observed the seventh day as the Sabbath. They rested no other day. *Luther's Fore-Runners*, pp.7, 8. [1]

Come Ye Yourselves Apart

Eleventh Century A.D.

"Margaret of Scotland in 1060 attempted to bring ruin to Columba's spiritual descendants by moving against those who observed the seventh-day Sabbath instead of Sunday." Reported by T.R. Barnett in *Margaret of Scotland, Queen and Saint*, p. 97. [2]

Twelfth Century A.D.

France: "For twenty years Peter de Bruys stirred southern France. He especially emphasized a day of worship that was recognized at that time among the Celtic churches of the British Isles, among the Paulicians, and in the great Church of the East, namely, that seventh day of the fourth commandment." J. F. Coltheart, *The Sabbath of God Through the Centuries*, p. 18. [1]

Thirteenth Century A.D.

"The Paulicians, Petrobusians, Passaginians, Waldenses, Insabbatati were great Sabbath-keeping bodies of Europe down to 1250 A.D." *Ibid.*, p. 19. [1]

Fourteenth Century A.D.

"In 1320, two hundred years before Luther's theses, the Bohemian brethren constituted one-fourth of the population of Bohemia... Erasmus pointed out how strictly Bohemian Waldenses kept the seventh day Sabbath." Armitage, *A History of the Baptists,* p. 313; Robert Cox, *The Literature of the Sabbath Question*, Volume 2, pp. 201, 202. [1]

Fifteenth Century A.D.

"Erasmus testifies that even as late as about 1500 these Bohemians not only kept the seventh day scrupulously, but were also called Sabbatarians." R. Cox, *ibid.* [1]

Sixteenth Century A.D.

Abyssinia: "It is not, therefore, in imitation of the Jews, but in obedience to Christ and His holy apostles, that we observe the day

Appendix

[the Sabbath]." From an Abyssinian legate at the court of Lisbon, 1534, quoted in Geddes's *Church History of Ethiopia*, pp. 87, 88. [1]

"The Sabbatarians teach that the outward Sabbath, i.e. Saturday, still must be observed. They say that Sunday is the Pope's invention." *Refutation of Sabbath,* by Wolfgang Capito, Published 1599. [1]

"The observance of the Sabbath is a part of the moral law. It has been kept holy since the beginning of the world." Ref. Noted Swiss writer, R. Hospinian, 1592. [1]

Seventeenth Century A.D.

"About 100 Sabbath keeping Churches, mostly independent, flourished in England in the 17th and 18th centuries." Dr. Brian W. Ball, *The Seventh-day Men, Sabbatarians, and Sabbatarianism in England and Wales,* 1600-1800, Clarendon Press, Oxford University 1994. [It must also be noted that the Sabbath was also kept in other parts of Europe and in America at this same time.] [2]

"It will surely be far safer to observe the seventh day, according to express commandment of God, than on the authority of mere human conjuncture to adopt the first [day]." John Milton, *Sabbath Literature 2,* pp. 46-54. [1]

Eighteenth Century A.D.

"Before Zinzendorf and the Moravians at Bethlehem [Pennsylvania] thus began the observance of the Sabbath and prospered, there was a small body of German Sabbath-keepers in Pennsylvania." *Rupp's History of the Religious Denominations in the United States,* pp. 109-123. [1]

Count Zinzendorf said of himself in 1738: "That I have employed the Sabbath for rest for many years already..." *Budingsche Sammlung,* Section 8, p. 224. Leipzig, 1742. [1]

Come Ye Yourselves Apart

As a special instance it deserves to be noticed that he [Zinzendorf] is resolved with the church at Bethlehem to observe the seventh day as [a] rest day." *Ibid.* pp. 5, 1421,1422.[1]

Nineteenth Century A.D.

China: "The Taipings when asked why they observed the seventh-day Sabbath, replied that it was, first, because the Bible taught it, and second, because their ancestors observed it as a day of worship." *A Critical History of Sabbath and the Sunday.* J. F. Coltheart, *The Sabbath of God through the Centuries*, p. 27. [1]

Twentieth Century A.D.

There were well over ten million Sabbath-keeping Christians worldwide among more than 25 denominations and hundreds of independent Sabbath-keeping congregations. Brian Jones, *A Time for Joy*, p. 21. [2]

Bibliography

All verses are taken from the King James Bible unless shown otherwise.

The Sabbath When Jesus Came

1.) Stein, Jess. *The Random House Dictionary of the English Language College Edition,* (New York, Random House, 1968) under "fulfill" definition 2

Origin of Christian Sunday Worship

1.) http://en.wikipedia.org/wiki/Sol_Invictus#Constantin

2.) Translated by Henry Percival. From Nicene and Post-Nicene Fathers, Second Series, Vol. 14. Edited by Philip Schaff and Henry Wace. (Buffalo, NY: Christian Literature Publishing Co., 1900.) Revised and edited for New Advent by Kevin Knight. http://www.newadvent.org/fathers/3806.htm).

3.) Geiermann, Rev. Peter, C.SS.R. *The Convert's Catechism of Catholic Doctrine,* (St. Louis, B. Herder Book Co., 1946) p. 50

4.) *Rome's Challenge,* (Cannon Falls, Master Books) p. 32

5.) Coltheart, Elder J. F. *The Sabbath of God Through the Centuries,* (Angwin, L. L .T. Productions, 1954) p. 27.

Come Ye Yourselves Apart

6.) Stein, Jess. *The Random House Dictionary of the English Language College Edition*, (New York, Random House, 1968) under Constantine I.

It is Finished

1.) White, Ellen, *Present Truth*, "The Sufferings of Christ" 1886

2.) White, Ellen, *Desire of Ages*, "Calvary" (Mountain View, Pacific Press Publishing Association 1898) p. 756

Forthright Admissions

1.) Jones, Brian. *A Time for Joy*, (Family Heritage Books, 1998) 22, 23.

2.) Coltheat, Elder J. F. *The Sabbath of God Through the Centuries*, (Angwin, L. L. T. Productions, 1954) pp. 23, 27.

3.) *Rome's Challenge*, (Cannon Falls, Master Books) pp. 2, 3, 5, 25, 26, 27

4.) Barrett, David V. *The New Believers: A Survey of Sects, Cults and Alternative Religions*, (Cassell & Co Wellington House, London, 2001, distributed in the United Sates of America by Sterling Publishing Co., Inc., New York) p. 126.

Appendix

1.) Coltheart, Elder J. F. *The Sabbath of God Through the Centuries*, (Angwin, L. L .T. Productions, 1954)

2.) Jones, Brian. *A Time for Joy*, (Family Heritage Books, 1998) pp. 20, 21.